29931

THE HIERARCHY OF HELL

By the same author

VIET-NAM
BENEDICT ARNOLD: *Hero and Traitor*
WARM BEER AND COLD COMFORT
BOLIVAR THE LIBERATOR
A GAGGLE OF GHOSTS
WITCHES IN FACT AND FANTASY
SEX IN WITCHCRAFT

THE HIERARCHY
OF HELL

LAURAN PAINE

ROBERT HALE · LONDON

PRINTED IN GREAT BRITAIN BY
CLARKE, DOBLE & BRENDON LTD.
PLYMOUTH

Contents

Illustrations

ONE

The Concepts of Hell

The concept of Hell appears in the earliest thought of man, along with a concept of varying kinds of an antithesis, Heaven, exactly as a concept of epitomized good, or God, appears as the antithesis of evil, the Devil.

The duality of man perhaps encouraged a conviction that good and evil existed everywhere, in all things, or speculating beyond the mists, such ideas may have arisen from a duality in Nature, i.e., the sun bringing light and warmth was good, the moon, the lord of darkness because it brought fear and cold and sightlessness, was evil.

Whatever the origin, Hell came into the Christian theology, not in an original form, but already fashioned and sustained by thousands of years of ceaseless forming, and, like much else in Christian theology, was pagan in origin yet suitable in both theory and practice. The need of relatively modern man was little different from the need of ancient man. Both understood that there *was* evil, along with non-evil, and had to hypothesize a place, a hell, where evil, when it was cast out, could be consigned; and both shared a belief that evil, requiring punishment, could not be allowed in that Other Place, that serene Heaven, where goodness was rewarded.

Hell had to be as terrifying as imagination could make it. But imagination was limited by the vistas of the mind. In other words, when man fantasized devils, they had grotesque but recognizable forms; they had bodies like man, or wolves, or serpents, and their expressions were frightful, but each face, mutilated, altered, exaggerated, *was a face*; thus Hell was never inhabited by really unimaginable things, even though some said this was so, because the restrictions of the imagination could not—and still cannot—

conceive of anything completely and truly imaginary; everything man conceives is from his personal prison—his earth-mind.

But that can be bad enough. Wolves, ancient man's foremost quadruped enemy, eaters of live or dead flesh, whose howls approximated the cries of the dead in torment and whose malevolent eyes glowed red in the firelight beyond the cave's opening, were for thousands of years a source of incarnate evil. Lyncanthropy evolved, devils as men being transformed into wolves.

Hell had wolves. It also had even more frightful demons: serpents. But the serpents of Hell could not be simple vipers. They were enlarged, armoured, thrice-fanged; they became winged and taloned, practically indestructable, highly intelligent, evil dragons, but the original concept was a worm.

The ancient Egyptians, borrowing from earlier peoples whose ideas certainly came from nature, had Osiris and Ra as their lords of Heaven, and Set, the malignant adversary of Horus, as their devil.

The dead belonged in spirit (soul) to Osiris in Heaven, but the natural body in its grave could not be taken up. It lay defenceless against the organic hunger of earth, its principal enemy worms. The Egyptians symbolized death as a worm, which evolved into a serpent that was hostile to the dead. In the Pyramid of Unas was a diorama and a recital, or charm, intended to protect the deceased from serpents, meaning worms.

Again, ancient man saw worms as representative of the evil, the life-dissolving, force. The Egyptians of 6000 B.C. only elaborated on what they had borrowed, and the Christians, not actually fearful of death and therefore probably capable of evolving something better, did not do so, and the worm-serpent passed into their theology scarcely altered. Even the Copts, Christian Egyptians, retained this symbol of Set, of evil, and they knew its pagan origin, which most Christians did not.

So serpents as metamorphosed worms, entered Hell without any opposition, first in the crude theology of near-men, later in the sophisticated faith of those who, like the Egyptians, evolved a state-faith, and finally into the religions of modern man.

The Egyptians of later times, from their eighteenth dynasty forward, improved on an earlier concept of Hell, called Taut, or Tat, and ruled by Taut, the Devil. Taut was not like the Hebrew

Sheol or Jehannum or the Christian Hell; it was that other place where the dead-departed went after life and where Tauti or lesser spirits ruled, under the spirit, Tuaut. Although the literal meaning of the word Taut has long been lost, it would seem that, although Taut was similar to the form by which it was eventually adopted into Hebrew and Christian theology, it was not, in the Egyptian context, a place where only the evil went for punishment, but was rather where all departed spirits went, and where *only* the evil were made to suffer.

At any rate, Taut was a dismal place. Its full panoply is lost but enough remains. According to Sir Wallis Budge in his *The Book the Dead*, "The Taut was divided into twelve parts, corresponding to the twelve hours of the night. . . . In one of these divisions, which was under the rule of the god Seker, the entrance was guarded by a serpent on four legs with a human head, and within were a serpent with three heads, scorpions, vipers, and winged monsters of terrifying aspect; a vast desert place was their abode, and seemingly the darkness was so thick there that it might be felt. In other divisions we find serpents spitting fire, lions, crocodile-headed gods, a serpent that devours the dead, a huge crocodile, and many other reptiles of divers shapes and forms."

Later concepts of Hell enlarged upon the torment, the darkness, the dire punishment, but not so much that the earlier Egyptian and much earlier prehistoric ideas were not recognizable. In theory, Hell evolved right along with man. It changed as the eras and epochs of man changed, in exactly the same way that man's gods or God changed. The four-legged serpent of Seker became under Christianity a scaly dragon, a rough-textured winged devil, but in purpose it remained unrelenting and ominous.

Taut gave way to other names. The term 'hell' has an affinity to 'hole', meaning a cavern, a dark, unpleasant place; *helan* or *behelian*. It was the Hebrew Sheol or Gehenna or the Greek Hades and Tartaros.

In the Septuagint and the New Testament the Hebrew term Sheol appears as Hades, meaning a dim, shadowy region where the dead, by some means, continued to exist. It was, rather like Taut (probably where the idea came from), the destination of good and bad alike and was not viewed as an exclusive place of punishment (Job, iii, 13–19). Thus the Hebrew Sheol is almost identical to the Greek Hades, in turn derived from the older concepts already cited.

In the apocryphal and apocalyptic books, finally, the idea was reshaped to another time, and to a fresh layer of religious thought and philosophy. Hell emerged as a place where moral qualities had a reward for the good, punishment and damnation for the bad. The distinction, not altogether clear in some earlier theologies, was clearly set forth in the New Testament.

Shoel (Septuagint: Hades) has been translated as 'grave' or 'pit' in the King James version, but although King James' version was for centuries a leading inspiration, its sponsor was a superstitious and biased man, and his 'version' abounds in errors. Nonetheless, Hades became Hell. The American Revised Version throughout simply copies the original words, reserving such designations as Gehenna and Tartaros for historic form, using Hell by preference. The Greek Tartaros refers to the locality beneath Hades where, according to the Homeric classics, supernatural troublemakers were confined.

In the Apocrypha and New Testament the modern version of Hell as a place of misery firms up, but precise references to the location are vague. Dante's *Inferno* and similar gloomy imaginings have had to particularize because the New Testament failed to utilize a grisly doom for sinners as a religious motive, even though mentioning the frightful suffering and loss—claimed by many New Testament authors to be permanent. Very little more could be claimed on scriptural authority.

It was, of course, both a curse and a blessing, a curse because Christians, confused about Hell, could only *fear* it without understanding it. A blessing because the Roman Catholic and Greek Churches were free to shape the idea according to their needs. Indeed, the idea of Purgatory as a place of purification for some of the faithful who died in sin was a doctrine instituted by Catholic theologians, while repudiation of this doctrine formed an element of Protestantism, generally.

Other Christian theories of Hell included one associated with the name of Origen. It was termed either Larger Hope, Universalism, or Restoration, and had to do with the idea that all men will ultimately be saved. Origen thought that Hell's torment was purgatorial in character, and that when its purifying effect had been achieved, punishment would cease. This, the theory of *Apocatastasis*, was a favourite among the humanitarian early Christian writers. It was believed by Gregory of Nyssa, who told of a time when "there shall no longer be a sinner in the Universe, and the war between good and evil shall be ended".

But not everyone accepted the Catholic Hell nor the Catholic Purgatory. For 1,000 years after the passing of Christ scattered Scandinavians clung to old Norse mythology. Hel to these people did not mean the underworld of Homer. Hel was the ill-favoured goddess of a gloomy place, which was the Norse underworld. Norsemen who fell in battle went to Valhalla, all others went down to Hel's underworld. But this realm of Hel was not a place of torment and punishment as much as it was a place for the dead to wait for judgment; if they were evil, only then did they suffer.

The Christian Hell also borrowed some of this mythology in its early days. Hell had four divisions. The first one was reserved for punishment of demons as well as men; this was the domain of the damned. The second division was for infants who died guiltless except for the original sin, and the presumption was that, after some mild form of punishment, these dead would not remain in Hell. Another division was a similar limbo; here the souls of those who died before Christ had to wait admission to Heaven until they could be enlightened. The fourth division was Purgatory of the Catholics; here the just who had died in venial sin were purified through suffering before being admitted to Heaven.

The idea of Hell as being an underworld came from earliest man, was adopted by later man, and passed without dispute into modern, contemporary theology for the same basic reason earliest man created his dark, fearful, mysterious and unknown underworld—because the dead *went down into the earth*, the mystery of their passing incomprehensible. Death was an inevitable event. From prehistoric times to the present, no man ever resolved its riddle although its occurrence was constant, thousands of times every day between sunrise and sunset.

Death was darkness, it was a void, all feeling stopped with its coming, those who experienced it were changed forever. The people who struggled hardest against it, who mummified corpses and evolved involved rituals to mitigate it, did not alter its arrival nor its course by so much as one ten-thousandth of a second; and although some zealot priests hallucinated about it, seeing past death, those who were rational, even among the most superstitious races, recognized the complete finality of it, and so buried the dead, filling the earth with their departed, putting them *down*. And *down* became the dark place, *down* was below the earth; the evil dead went farther down—to Hell—thus *Hell* and *down* became synonymous.

Enlightened people worked out a justification for *down*, but only because in the remembering soul the lingering fear survived. The Latin *infernus* includes the element *in*; therefore the implication is that the *infernus*, the inferno, is *in* the earth. The Hebrew Sheol, corresponding to Hell, probably in its original context referred to something hollow or sunken, the kingdom of the dead, for the good as well as the bad, but in any case *down, below*. It was Hell. The Greek Hades, like Hebrew Sheol, relates to the common word Hell.

Christ's ascension, for Christians at least, lifted the ancient essence of limbo. Henceforth *up* was Heaven, or salvation, but *down* or *below* remained as the Other Place, except that, with no one any longer in limbo, those who resided in Hell had to be only the damned. All others by-passed the ancient void of limbo and went directly to Heaven. It made for a tidier theology.

But the prehistoric superstition remained: *down* into the grave corresponded to the same fear and dread. It had simply emerged anew, a more sophisticated hypothesis, supported by written language. The same craft enabled theologians to up-grade the old universal term; Hell did not vanish at all, but in the New Testament the term Gehenna (Hebrew: *Ĝehinnom, ĝe-ben-hinnom*) referred to the underworld of punishment, little different from the much earlier Jehannum.

Gehenna probably derived from Gehinnom, the Valley of Hinnom south of Jerusalem where in early time an abomination, the worship of Moloch, occurred, and afterwards was defiled by Josias (IV Kings, xxii, 10), cursed by Jeremiah (Jeremiah, vii, 31–3) and was held by the Hebrews to be an abode of the damned.

The *idea* of Hell did not change much, but, according to both early and late epochs, its name, even its location, frequently changed. The Gehenna of the New Testament came from a valley where evil had arisen, or it was a place somewhere below the earth—or below the world itself—where darkness thick enough to feel endured eternally.

Biblical chroniclers, the early Hebrews, the still earlier Egyptians, had ways of commemorating their ideas on papyrus or stone, but their concepts of Hell came in full essence from much earlier animists who had no written language.

And Hell there always was, a dark projection of the evil latent in the duality of man, representative of it. It was given form and substance as the evil as well as the good in man progressed from animism to paganism, to Christianity and its additional fresh theologies, each a new layer to conform to a new time, but fundamentally identifiable with the earlier forms, and actually no better although more sophisticated. As with the concept of Hell, the domain—or the prison—of man, his mind, can neither conceive of anything better, nor if real comprehension obtained, understand it.

Thus Hell, the entire theological achievement man-made from the beginning, is not amenable to radical change—unless man undergoes radical change. As for Hell, most of the imagining has been accomplished. The worst that can befall man is only the worst that he can imagine in his separate environments. Basically, Hell must be a frightening place, dark because man is most helpless in darkness, full of physical agony because man dreads physical pain. From these bases can be built a most harrowing underworld, but always Hell has to be inhabited only by familiar or semifamiliar things, as though God and Satan, its creators, were as restricted in their ingenuity as man himself.

As a motive for religion, for leading a decent life, Hell had no equal. Luke, xvi, 28, calls it a "place of torments". In Matthew, xiii, 42 and 50 it is a "furnace of fire". In Matthew, viii, 12; xxii, 13; xxv, 30; Hell is an "outer darkness". As the place of the damned it is called "destruction" and "perdition", "eternal destruction", and "corruption". Every designation is employed to strike fear into Christian hearts.

Whether Hell as a Christian adoptive was ever equal to the demands made upon it is questionable. Christians for 2,000 years shuddered at the prospect of damnation, but as a sect behaved no differently than pre-Christian peoples to whom Hell meant

B

basically the same thing. Also, Hell could be brought to earth—as in the genocide-like murder of something in the region of half a million people accused, tortured, and burned at the stake as witches during the Middle Ages, for the salvation of their souls and to the Glory of God; or, well within the recollection of living men, the equally barbarous mass-murder of 6 million European Jews, Poles, and Russians, without even the same pretences.

TWO

The Location of Hell

The specific locality of Hell has never been constant. The Egyptian Hell—by any name, but usually Amenti—was a great cavern, the 'Hall of Truth', where the dead were judged in the presence of Osiris and forty-two underworld assessors, the 'Lords of Truth'. Anubis, the son of Osiris, 'the director of the weight', using delicate scales, put in one the symbol of Truth, in the other one a vase containing the good deeds of the deceased. Thoth, standing nearby with a tablet, recorded the results. If the good deeds were heaviest the deceased was conducted, by boat, to Aahlu, the 'Pools of Peace', dwelling place of the blessed. If the good deeds were insufficient to sway the balance, the deceased had to begin a transmigration through animal bodies. But if, at a final judgment by Osiris, the deceased was found incurable or unamenable, he was then sentenced to complete annihilation at the hands of Shu, the 'Lord of Light', upon the steps of Heaven. Except for a vague reference, the locality of this 'Hall of Truth' was not defined.

The Assyrians and Babylonians also had a Hell, but it was not localized either. Beyond calling it a receptacle for the wicked after death, the place where "earth is men's food, and their nourishment clay; where light is not seen, but in darkness they dwell; where ghosts, like birds, flutter their wings, and on the door and doorposts the dust lies undisturbed", this "abode of darkness and famine" is not defined by locale.

In Assyrian theology there occurred a rebellion in Heaven when seven spirits created by Anu, a great lord of the universe, along with Bel launched a fierce attack, and after a prolonged period of hostility they were all cast out. These wicked angels flew to the lower world, there to remain, but again the location of this place, whose winged, fallen angels bear a distinct similarity to the fallen angels cast out of the Christian Heaven, was not defined.

The Chaldean goddess Ishtar—called Nana by the Babylonians and corresponding to the goddess Astarte of the Assyrians and Phoenicians—following the Deluge of Hea in the centuries before Christianity, descended to Hell and had to pass through seven gates to reach her destination. There, naked, she faced the wicked goddess of Hades, Nin-ki-gal, who derided her, while back in Heaven the god Hea, importuned by an assembly of deities, finally moved to rescue Ishtar, who had ". . . descended into the earth, and has not risen again. . .". Ishtar was returned to Heaven, but except for her having passed through seven gates and descending into the earth, where these things occurred was not given. (Ishtar, incidentally, was the very ancient predecessor of Aphrodite, and was worshipped by sexual orgies, called 'unchaste rites'; and her father was a god named Sin.)

Half a millennium before Christ, the Etruscans, whose religion was not dissimilar from that of other early ethnic groups, except that their particular deities—the Novensiles—were notable for making their presences known by hurling thunderbolts, devoted their chief concern to the place where mortals went after death. Here, below the earth, Etruscan spirits resided.

Over this realm of darkness ruled Mantus and Mania, king and queen of the dead, the former an old man, crowned and winged. The prime minister of the Etruscan Hades was a horrible creature, half-human, half-animal, whose cruelty was notorious. His name was Charun. He was described as an ogre-like individual with "flaming eyes and savage aspect", with "the ears and often the tusks of a brute . . . negro features and complexion . . . wings" and "cloven feet".

Charun corresponds to the Christian Satan, and since the Etruscans—or Tuscans—were settlers in early Italy, it is probable that their Charun became the Christian Satan, or at least lent some of his attributes to the Christian concept of Satan.

Charun stood by to receive the soul at death, put it upon a horse and escort it to Hades, where he and lesser demons of both sexes unmercifully beat and abused the soul. In fact the Etruscan version of the underworld seemed to correspond with other early underworlds inasmuch as, although it was a place of punishment, it was also where all the dead went, just and unjust, good and evil.

It would also appear that instead of a clear division of souls based on merit or otherwise, the Etruscans believed good and evil spirits contended over the dead. There did not seem to be any such rational ritual as that supervised by Osiris and his son Anubis in the Egyptian 'Hall of Truth'.

The departed Etruscan went to Heaven or Hell according to whether a good spirit or an evil one triumphed in the fierce but impersonal battle for his soul. Where this struggle occurred was open to question, but it was probably a desert. Specifically where this desert was, or which desert it might have been, no one ever knew.

Thousands of books were written on theology in early times and later, up to and including the twentieth century, but although punishment, torment and damnation are freely and energetically dealt with, and although all theologists devote time and space to Heaven, less than a fraction of them have made any attempt to define the location of Hell.

Many theologians defined Hell by its dreary or cruel aspect. Most seemed wary of going beyond those things; some said Hell was not a *place*, but a condition. It has been said that Hell is everywhere, including on earth, that the damned are at liberty to roam the entire universe, but always in torment and always carrying their anguish with them.

Those who have favoured this concept of Hell have been called Ubiquists or Ubiquitarians. Johann Brenz, the sixteenth-century German Protestant, was a strong exponent of this theory. Because it was consistent with the nature of man to consider restriction of movement as a form of punishment, Ubiquitarianism never achieved general popularity. Hell had to be a place where the damned were confined, their movements restricted as part of their punishment.

Early theologians who propounded the idea of Hell as a place of fire everlasting, while functioning according to Catholic and Protestant idealism, created a riddle no one could resolve. If Hell was a region of eternal fire, then obviously it could not be everywhere, i.e. on earth, particularly after the consummation of the world.

In former times it was possible to say—as some did—that Hell was located on a far island over the seas near the edge of the world. After there were few unexplored seas left, it was said that Hell was located either on top of the world, at the North Pole, or on the bottom, at the South Pole.

By the eighteenth century when it had to be moved again, an Englishman, Swinden, gave it a more reasonable location—the sun. This opened up an entirely new vista; Mars and the moon were suggested. Not many theologians and even fewer laymen were convinced Hell was on Mars; and the American lunar landings turned up the fact that although at one time, in the millennia of the past, the moon had indeed been red-hot, it is not so any longer.

Holy Writ is vague; it appears to concede that Hell is within the earth. Hell, says the Bible, is an abyss into which the wicked descend. In some places (Numbers, xvi, 30; Ezekiel, xxvi, 20; Philippians, ii, 10), there is mention made of the earth opening up to receive the damned. In a metaphorical sense this is reasonable: God is in Heaven, the wicked, human and otherwise, should be confined as far from Him as possible, thus their abode, Hell, would be below Heaven. Light, as evinced in the splendour of the skies has long been a reflection of God's glory throughout the firmament. Hell, therefore, because it was an antithesis of Heaven, had not only to be remote, it had also to be dark, and the damned, being completely estranged from God, could not share in any way in His glory, in the splendour of Heaven, or in the serenity of eternal peace.

The Church sanctioned this much, but took no official position on the specific location of Hell, although theologians, traditionally choosing to follow Holy Writ, wrote of Hell as being within the earth. Metaphor permitted a wide latitude, but churchmen of the orthodox persuasions preferred the Bible verbatim; when it was written that the wicked *descended* into Hell, into the earth which opened up to receive them, orthodox opinion held that Hell *was a place*, and that it was *within the earth*.

Where, within the earth, this dark place of fire everlasting and eternal torment might be located, was not said. "We must not ask", said St. Chrysostom, "where Hell is, but how we are to escape it." St. Augustine was also circumspect on this issue: "It

is my opinion that the nature of hell-fire and the location of hell
are known to no man unless the Holy Ghost made it known to
him by a special revelation." Nevertheless, St. Augustine thought
Hell was beneath the earth. St. Gregory said, "I do not dare to
decide this question. Some thought hell is somewhere on earth;
others believe it is under the earth."

Under the earth ceased to be a practical place for the location
of Hell when the science of astronomy proved the earth was not
stationary. This did not entirely preclude Hell as an orbital satellite
revolving with earth, in some degree of proximity, but it promoted
a reasonable degree of justifiable scepticism.

The Age of Reason made refutation relatively easy for those
unwilling to accept the idea that Hell could be a uniquely restricted dependency of earth, a form of exclusive hot place that
hovered in an eternal shadow below a moving world for the
purpose of raking off a surplus of wicked human beings. In fact
the Age of Reason, in its impatience and intolerance, cast serious
doubts on the wickedness of humanity. Without seeming to rely
on any of the older theses, it was more indebted to Aristippus
of Cyrene—who died more than three centuries before the
Christian advent—than to its more noted protagonist, Thomas
Paine. Its latter-day variety of hedonism held that pain was the
greatest evil, not sin; that truth exists simply in relation to each
individual, not the whole; and that universal truth and good are
impossible. Thus Hell, even as a place, was doubtful and debat-
able. But whether it actually existed, as the Church said, or did
not exist, the possibility of it being under the moving world was
not simply unlikely, it was liable to ridicule.

The learned theologians who chose a reasonably factual interpretation of Holy Writ remained, of all others, still unshakable;
Hell was indeed *within the earth*.

If, as science postulates, the earth's core is molten, then it
may be a fair hypothesis that the location of Hell is at the core
of—not the *under*world, but the *inner*world, as these stubborn
theologians have maintained for many centuries. However, as Hell
was movable in the past it may be transferable again, whenever
human ingenuity makes exploration of the earth's centre feasible.

The *fact* of Hell has always been more amenable to reason than
the *location* of Hell. Most religions have had predictions concern-

ing the after-life of those who have died in mortal personal sin, and who, as enemies of God, are unworthy of eternal salvation, but not all have been willing to lay original sin upon the newborn. In fact not all have been agreeable to the theory and practice of Hell. Pantheists and materialists in recent centuries, as well as Jews and Gnostics and Sadducees, among others, in former times—contrary to Catholic insinuation that those who deny Hell also of necessity deny God—doubted the existence of Hell.

Even those churchmen who would not be drawn out on the location of Hell, were unanimous in teaching that the wicked would be punished after death. The Athanasian Creed to which the Roman Church adhered, said in part that, "They that have done good shall go into life everlasting, and they that have done evil, into everlasting fire." At both the Council of Lyons and the Council of Florence, it was noted that "the souls of those who depart in mortal sin, or only in original sin, go down immediately into Hell, to be visited . . . with unequal punishment".

Thus it has usually required no more than a statement of fact, based upon the need of social-man to obey laws, for the logic of Hell to seem reasonable. The good are rewarded, the evil are punished; the reward, of itself, appeals to those who, knowing as much about afterlife as theologians know—nothing at all—are hopeful, while the blackmail of Hell—a place as sinister as imagination can conceive—frightens all others.

It is a unique element of human nature that of those things which we know the least, we can imagine most, and it is part of our subconscious hope that supplies from within that which our senses do not supply from without. Thus we can very handily, once we accept the theory of Hell, imagine the grisly and terrifying practice of it. But as it grows in imagination, it also becomes unamenable to specifics. As a living nightmare it can no more be fit into the world of the five senses than can most other nightmares. It cannot be brought to earth, so it exists beyond, or below, or within, and if the devout are susceptible to literal translation, even though most others are of necessity vague about the location of Hell, the devout will continue to believe that Hell *is a place within the earth*.

THREE

The Eternity of Hell

Until a rather general adoption of monotheism, or the acceptance of one highest and eternal deity by most of mankind, the *human* god or gods which had previously prevailed made it possible for polytheism to be a reflection of man in whose likeness these human gods were fashioned—rather than *vice versa*, as in Christianity—with the result that human gods were vulnerable. They upon occasion were demoted, banished, even killed, and rather often they were even exiled to Hades, a result of creating gods who were as susceptible to misfortune as were men.

On the other hand there was an advantage to this system that held misfortune and travail to be transitory: the damned were rarely *eternally* damned. As in historic Egyptian theology, previously cited, those sent below for punishment could work their way through transmigration back to acceptability.

Not many ancient faiths were addicted to everlasting torment. As with the early Greeks, whose religion was muscular and generally pleasant, the idea of everlasting anguish was illogical. Man's existence was neither constantly pleasant nor unpleasant, therefore neither was the existence of his gods. Nothing, actually, lasted forever, nor should anything last forever. Gods created in the likeness of men were not invulnerable because neither was their prototype.

It did not harm the god-man relationship to have these human-god-types serve as a reflection of man, although very often it encouraged a familiarity that a monotheistic faith such as Christianity did not tolerate. The human god was propitiated about as often as he was revered, and upon occasion he fell from favour rather resoundingly.

From this kind of a basis it was reasonable for polytheists to

believe in the existence of Hell while simultaneously denying the
eternity of its punishment. The Conditionalists—Gnostics *et al*—
who believed wicked souls merited punishment, and whose faith
rejected anything but a hypothetical immortality, thought that
punishment was temporary and that the incorrigibly damned were
annihilated.

Some more recent theologians have taught that all the damned
will ultimately achieve beatitude, but this is an old option. St.
Augustine spoke of it. Scotus Eriugena (or Erigena) believed it.
Going as far back as religious philosophy leads, the idea of a
limited period of punishment prevailed, probably as much because
the old-time human gods and their intransigence made it appear
probable, as because rational theologians and philosophers
appeared irreconcilable to an idea that for whatever crime a man
could possibly commit on earth, fire, torment, everlasting punishment was intolerable.

Most rationalists, even a few Catholics (Schell and Hirscher),
have sought to mitigate the idea of Hades as a place where
Christians must spend all eternity undergoing the most un-
Christian agonies, by borrowing a little from some benign old
pagans. Those who do not die in the state of grace, according to
these authorities, can still be converted after death, if they are not
too impenitent and wicked. This is the same idea, in essence, as
the ancient Egyptians had.

But Hell *is* eternal. The punishment of the damned shall be
forever and ever. It is to be as everlasting as are the joys of
Heaven (Matthew, xxv, 46). In Mark, ix, 43, 44 Jesus said, ". . . go
into hell, into the fire that never shall be quenched: Where their
worm dieth not, and the fire is not quenched." For Christians
the fire and anguish of Hell is repeatedly referred to as eternal
and everlasting. ". . . the wrath of God abideth on him" (John,
iii, 36) who does not acknowledge Christ, and everlasting hell-fire
is his punishment.

The Athanasian Creed sets forth the Catholic Church's position, and so does the common liturgy: damnation is forever, and
the church may not offer prayers for the damned. According to
The Catholic Encyclopedia, ". . . the Church expressly teaches
the eternity of the pains of Hell as a truth of faith which no
one can deny or call in question without manifest heresy".

Protestants have historically held an identical view. Buddhists, too, have a permanent Hades, but their Hell is divided into eight sections, each more terrible than its predecessor, and while the wicked can be purged in sections one through seven, the eighth section—where heretics, but more commonly wicked souls who have not been liberal in their offerings to Buddhist priests on earth, are confined—is where the wicked will rot forever.

Generally, though, eternal damnation has not been popular, and the reason seems to be that, contrary to the Christian view that "although the act of sinning is brief, the guilt of sin remains forever", centuries of logicians have preferred to believe that there has never been a crime men could commit that would warrant such unrelenting punishment. Further, the fact that reasonable punishment for varying periods, depending upon the sin, could ensure redemption, has long had merit in many different ages and parts of the world.

Those whose unrelenting zeal adhered to the word of Holy Writ have said that reason cannot "give any conclusive proof for the eternity of the pains of hell, but that it can . . . show that this doctrine does not involve any contradiction". These theologians have also maintained that any idea claiming that the purpose of punishment was to reform the evil-doers is false because aside from torment inflicted for the purpose of correction, there is an even more stern injunction which involves the satisfaction of justice: ". . . justice demands that whoever departs from the right way in his search for happiness shall not find happiness, but shall lose it. The eternity of the pains of Hell responds to this demand of justice."

Very little opposition has historically or currently arisen against the idea of Hell and punishment. Aside from assorted holy works, all of which threaten transgressors with punishment in after-life, the basis for earthly social existence requires that people living together do so amicably, if possible, for otherwise anarchy ensues. Punishment is the reward for criminals on earth. It has always been. When early man conceived his theology and breathed life into it, he knew only the rules that worked best for him in his village, so he instilled them into his religion, and ever after other social animals residing together adopted, and adapted, them.

But the concept of Hell, while it was assumed to be a permanent place, did not as a rule include ideas about perpetual torture. At this juncture many ancient religions departed from the Christian concepts. Even some contemporary religions rejected this manifest barbarity, preferring not to accept the orthodox view that "The damned are confirmed in evil; every act of their will is evil and inspired by hatred of God". Some who have not opposed this edict, have on the other hand, pointed out that a god as willing to forgive as is the Christian God, or at least as the Bible professes that He is, would not only understand that hatred being the only motivation for the very wicked, had unbalanced them, but would also understand that partial damnation, for a shorter period of time than all eternity, would certainly ensure that sinners could be redeemed.

But Christianity was not a religion of compromise, and for as many centuries as militant Catholicism was the sole representative of God on earth, the idea of an eternity of Heaven and an eternity of Hell endured. St. Thomas taught that the major cause of damnation was the varieties of impenitence that divine justice could not excuse, and would not extend grace to; thus the damned were doomed for all eternity.

It was also said, as another example of the need for a permanent Hades, that because the damned were unable to show any emotion towards God but hatred, redemption and conversion were impossible. Also, that their free choice of a life of wickedness and impenitence, a state of sin which they voluntarily chose on earth, rendered them entirely unfit even for such a place as purgatory where those dying in grace sojourned until, properly expiated, they could be received in Heaven, because the truly wicked person was too far gone in corruption to be admissable in any hereafter excepting Hell everlasting.

Those choosing to question this uncompromising attitude did so on the grounds that since earthly evil could hardly inconvenience a celestial universe, and the worst sin of mankind could not exceed a physical limitation, such ruthless punishment was excessive.

Orthodox theologians answered that the damned did not incur any increase in their torment-everlasting as God-haters on earth, or as secular aberrants. God warned all men, many times over, that the reward of evil was everlasting damnation, and if those who made the free choice embraced evil, they knew the penalty. Furthermore, it would not only be intrinsically impossible for God to move the damned to repentance, it would also be impolitic for Him to pronounce unequivocally for punishment everlasting, and then to abrogate it.

Unlike Osiris, the Christian God did not "consider the eternal punishment of Hell as a series of separate or distinct terms of punishment, as if God were forever and again pronouncing" a new judgment. "Hell is, especially in the eyes of God, one and indivisible in its entirety; it is but one sentence and one penalty."

Nor did Christianity's God liberate souls from Hell, even though some said this occurred (Peter, i, 9). The legend of Gregory the Great praying the Emperor Trajan out of Hell has been branded an untrustworthy misinterpretation of facts by the Catholic Church.

Sin is an offence against the authority of God; sinners, even those who do not comprehend the magnitude of sin, are to some degree aware that they are in defiance of Him. These people, those who understand the penalty and those who only vaguely or imperfectly believe there is a penalty for wickedness, are equally liable to eternal damnation for their malice.

In its perseverence, the Christian dedication to everlasting Hell over the centuries met all objections with an unyielding adamancy. Sinners, it consistently held, lost the beatific vision; they had been so alienated in body and soul that their separation from God prevented them from knowing Him even in their moments of peace and rest. This loss of faith was accompanied by a loss of all supernatural conviction; they became either atheists with contempt for God, or they became revilers, scorners, sufferers, even in the midst of their material pleasures, envious of those who found serenity in Christianity.

For God to reveal Himself to such individuals, said learned theologians, would be to permit them to glimpse true happiness, which they did not deserve. This was the *poena damni*, the pain of loss. It was said to be at the very foundation of damnation—those who lost God were doomed, there was no way for them to be redeemed. Furthermore, at the core of every sin could be found some degree of this loss of feeling and identity with God and righteousness. If a Christian persevered in sin, eventually the malice in his spirit would triumph, he would become wicked, pain of loss would ensue, and ultimately the reward of sin would be eternal damnation.

In earlier times quite a few complex religions existed, but in the eras of pre-science when very little was known of natural law and natural phenomena, mythology served rather admirably. Up until the era of earliest Christianity, in fact for several centuries after the Crucifixion, mythology still throve; but probably could not have existed unchanged subsequent to the advent of Christ—not because of Him—but because as man evolved, learned, progressed, his concepts changed. The more advanced the people, the fewer the gods, and mythology had hordes of gods.

Christianity was the proper Western faith for its time. Its complexity—which was never Christ's doing—equalled any of those more ancient faiths, as time passed becoming even more elaborately complex than most old-time pagan religions.

It required 1,000 years for answers to be evolved for such questions as those concerning the need for everlasting hell-fire, for logic to be coerced into a semblance of reason in order that an eternal Hades could be acceptably justified. But Christianity never lacked for zealots. No state religion ever lacked for advocates.

The hell-fire dictum of early paganism, denounced as Satan's villainy by Christians encountering it in the fetishist faiths of ancient people, became for Christians the *poena sensus*, or pain of sense, no different in purpose or function, but eminently more reasonable and respectable under the Jesus aegis.

In *The Catholic Encyclopedia*, Father Joseph Hontheim, S.J., Professor of Dogmatic Theology at St. Ignatius College, Valkenburg, Holland, explained the *poena sensus*:

> The . . . pain of sense, consists in the torment of fire so frequently mentioned in Holy Writ. According to the greater number of theologians the term *fire* denotes a material fire, and so a real fire. . . . Some few of the Fathers also thought of a metaphorical explanation. Nevertheless, Scripture and tradition speak again and again of the fire of Hell, and there is no sufficient reason for taking the term as a mere metaphor. It is urged: How can a material fire torment demons, or human souls before the resurrection of the body? But if our soul is so joined to the body as to be keenly

sensitive to the pain of fire, why should the omnipotent God be unable to bind even pure spirits to some material substance in such a manner that they may suffer torment more or less similar to the pain of fire which the soul can feel on earth? This reply indicates, as far as possible, how we may form an idea of the pain of fire which the demons suffer. . . . It is quite superfluous to add that the nature of Hell-fire is different from that of our ordinary fire; for instance it continues to burn without the need of a continually renewed supply of fuel. How are we to form a conception of that fire in detail remains quite undetermined; we merely know that it is corporeal. The demons suffer the torment of fire, even when, by Divine permission, they leave the confines of Hell and roam about on earth. In what manner this happens is uncertain. We may assume that they remain fettered inseparably to a portion of that fire—the pain of sense is the natural consequence of that inordinate turning to creatures which is involved in every mortal sin.

The pain of sense, combined with the pain of loss, then, constitute the basic anguish of the damned, with the *poena damni* being the worst. This is the very essence of everlasting torment, the pain of loss, the desolation of God's abandonment, which is eternal; and, because the agonies of Hell are immutable according to Christian theologists, there can be no interludes of mercy, and no alleviation.

"Hell", said Father Hontheim, "is a state of the greatest and most complete misfortune. After the last judgment there will be an increase of torment because subsequent to that event the demons and devils will never again be allowed to wander beyond the confines of Hell, and thus restricted, will have only the miserable souls of the damned to torture and torment throughout all eternity."

As late as the closing decade of the nineteenth century a prominent Christian theologian offered a hint of mitigation by suggesting that as time passed the punishment of the damned would be less until, thoroughly scourged—and presumably also purged—their condition would not be altogether dolorous, and in fact they might even dare hope for a kind of woebegone happiness. This was, of course, an up-dating of some of the very ancient pagan teachings, and it was to be expected that orthodox churchmen,

Protestant as well as Catholic, would at once and with consider-able zeal attack any such hypothesis.

They did, from all sides, driving the idea out altogether. Hades *is* eternal punishment. No less an authority than Holy Writ un-equivocally says as much. Any suggestion advocating anything less is heresy.

Upon this point innumerable Christians have faltered, and many a convert has baulked. Hell of the pantheists, of the fetishists, of the fire- and sky- and tree-worshippers, in fact the Hell of most heretical pagans of ancient or modern times, existed, not unlike the Hell of Christianity, even as an eternal place; but rarely were the damned condemned to spend time everlasting there without some chance of redemption, cruel and arduous though that redemption might be.

But the *eternity* of Hell was never in question. In fact the earliest worshippers, pantheists without exception, offered their fealty, not to God, but to demons and devils from Hell, with understandable logic. The benevolent gods were not to be feared, thus they could be treated as benign and quite often inept old grandfathers; but the shrieking devils who rode the lightning, directed thunder, guided floods and plagues and raging fires, had to be more circumspectly and fearfully acknowledged. The first human sacrifices were not made to God, they were made as propitiary offerings to devils whose home was in Hell..

Hades by all its various names down the ages, was never scorned, and few theologians, pagan or otherwise doubted its exist-ence. The gods changed. Prometheus who made man the gift of fire, degenerated into a devil, and Priapus, he of the eternal erec-tion, also ended in disrepute, as did the great god Poseidon; but Hades never languished, and as a repository for the fallen of all ages it was invaluable.

It was not important to make a distinction between religion and mythology in this context (if indeed there ever was any reason to make a distinction at all). Hell was constant. Regardless of the differences encountered respecting man's gods, his ideas of Hell were fundamentally the same. Further, in the historic sense, Hell has come down to present times more nearly pure in concept than any concept of religion. Hell has the distinction of never having had zealots to mar its perfection with warped logic. Satan has not suffered so badly at the hands of a Thomas Aquinas as has Christ.

Every religion must have its Hell and Satan, exactly as every religion must have its god and its serene hereafter. The religions have changed endlessly, but Hell as a place for the wicked has not, cannot, and very probably will not, change.

Interdenominational concurrence among theologians is rare. Even more impossible is concurrence between laymen of different faiths. But on the subject of Hell there has always been a uniformity of opinion. The practices may differ but the *purpose* never does. Hell is *there* and it is everlasting.

c

FOUR

The Devil's Image

The religious tenets and practices of nine principal faiths of antiquity, Egyptian, Etruscan, Phoenician, Sanskritic, Indian, Iranian, Assyrian, Babylonian, Greek and Roman—all the great nations with which ancient history is primarily concerned—had in common with the tenth nation of antiquity, Judea, a devil-image, different in many ways, frequently so in appearance and origin, but similar in function and purpose.

However, as in the case of ancient Egypt, the complexity of religious polytheism, founded in the practice of local gods and national gods bearing similar responsibilities and different names, or *vice versa*, made intelligible differentation almost impossible. One noted Egyptologist lists no fewer than seventy-three principal deities while another, equally qualified authority, lists sixty-three, and both note omissions although both also enumerate alternate names and functions for each god.

Osiris, the Egyptian lord of the dead—according to Plutarch— was put into bondage by Typhon, or Seth, the devil, and later was torn into fourteen parts by Seth (or Set). He is a fair example of what could happen to a god when his identity was subjected to a people who already had local gods when he appeared. Osiris became synonymous with Amen-Ra, Amen-Keph, Ra-Harmachis, Isis-Selk, Phthah-Sokari-Osiris, and so forth. About the only major Egyptian deity who managed to escape this variety of character fusing was Khem, lord of all generative power, representative of fecundity, growth and reproduction in nature, whose primary distinction was a great erect penis.

But Osiris as lord of Hades was rather a judge than a devil. The Egyptian pantheon had its separate, but not altogether disassociated demons. Set, also known as Sutech, Osiris's arch enemy (and also his brother) shown as a particularly ugly god with the head of a griffin or crocodile, was an implacable and powerfully malevolent demon and torturer. Associated with him was Bes, either a regional prototype of Set (Sutech or Typhon) or a separate deity, who was the god of death. Bes's wife or consort, Taouris, also a malevolent deity, and Apap, or Apepi, a great and evil serpent, constituted the most notable figures of ancient Egypt's Hell. (Apap was the serpent allegedly slain by Horus, son of Osiris.)

All of these malignant gods were represented as hideous and grotesque beings of the nether world, and although they were feared and hated, prudent Egyptians also worshipped them in the belief, as old as worship itself, that propitiation was a wise course. They built temples in their honour and wore personal charms whose purpose was to appease them. It was never the custom of ancient Egyptians to adopt the fiercely antagonistic attitude towards devils that the later Christians adopted. Their multiform religion was sufficiently bewildering to prompt caution, and yet most districts and towns usually revered only perhaps a triad of gods, or at least paid particular homage to a local triad, but willingly acknowledged the existence of the entire pantheon.

The devil-image of Set was part man, part beast, as devil images always have been. It was also an image of extreme cruelty, uncompromising evil, and unlimited and energetic vigour and vindictiveness. Set, as the Devil, was the personification of the principle of evil. The Egyptian religion, not unlike other contemporary and later religions, was dualistic. There was good and there was evil. Both were engaged in a constant, interminable struggle for supremacy, and while it was thought, or hoped, there might be a preponderance of good, it was so slight, if it existed, that no complete victory of good over evil was possible. But in earlier times Egyptians did not have any such clear-cut definition between good and evil; in those almost prehistoric times they apparently viewed the devil as part of the natural God, a view theologians have held at one time or another throughout the history of man down to and including the present time.

Set became a thorough demon only when the Egyptian evolution required it. Anu, or 'the old Anu', of Assyrian and Babylonian theology, known as 'the king of the lower world' and as 'the lord of spirits and demons', like the Egyptian's Set, appears on ancient

Chaldean tablets, not as a malevolent spirit except by implication. His symbol was a single wedge with the numerical power of
sixty. (Christianity's Satan had the numerical power of the number
666.)

But Anu, like the Assyrian and Babylonian Bel, eventually was
deprived of a special sphere and was categorized as simply a 'great
god', while Bel, noted in early mythology, became the ". . . god of
the lords", "the father of the gods", "the creator", and "the lord
of the world". He was the equivalent to Christianity's Supreme
Being, having created Heaven and Earth, and in forming man by
mixing his blood with earth. Bel was also the brother of Anu.
Their relationship was dualistic: Bel ordained and ruled an
orderly world, which he had created, while Anu was representative
of the primordial chaos, lord of all that lacked form and direction,
pointless matter.

Anu was different from Set, though, in that, as time passed,
while he changed, he did not become as hideously grotesque and
evil as did Set. Anu as an image of the lord of a nether world did
not become as fixed in an evil image as did, for example, the lesser
deity Iskalla, who dwelt in Hades, or the queen Nin-ki-gal, and
although Iskalla was feared his image was of a rather indifferent
lord of Hell. Even Nin-ki-gal (as in the legend of her spiteful
meeting with Sin's daughter, Ishtar) turned out to be a somewhat
relenting and easily influenced she-devil.

The Assyrian and Babylonian Hades was as gloomy as Hell has
always been, with a fair assortment of hideous creatures, torment,
fire and darkness, but its rulers did not emerge as more than recon-
dite images.

On the other hand Angro-Mainyus, lord of evil of the ancient
Iranians, was more recognizable for what he was. His name alone
was indicative of his character. Angro-Mainyus contains two
elements; an adjective and a substantive. 'Angro' was from
'niger or negro' meaning black. 'Mainyus', a substantive, is the
equivalent to the Latin 'mens', meaning mind or intelligence.
Angro-Mainyus meant black or evil intelligence.

Angro-Mainyus's opposite was the great god Ahura-Mazda,
creator of life, the holy god, the essence of truth, giver of all the
good that was in Heaven, earth, and in man.

These two battled constantly; whatever Ahura-Mazda created,

Angro-Mainyus tried to destroy. Angro-Mainyus's image was properly and believably evil. He was as vigorous as the Assyrian and Babylonian lords of darkness were obscure and vacillating. Where those other devils procrastinated, the Iranian lord of Hell and darkness was innovative and strong. Ahura-Mazda, the great good god could exert no control over Angro-Mainyus; even when they battled Ahura-Mazda was frequently bested. These two prototypes of eternal good and eternal evil divided between them the empire of the universe, their duality being the ancient— and modern—synthesis that has always prevailed in all places, in all times, among all men.

But Angro-Mainyus and Ahura-Mazda called into existence a legion of inferior spirits—demons—to assist them in the ever-lasting struggle. In the Zoroastrian system the leader of Ahura-Mazda's host was "the good, tall, fair Serosh" (Sraosha), who occupied the position later fulfilled under Christianity by the Archangel Michael. Angro-Mainyus's army of devils was super-vised but not commanded by the 'Bad Mind', Akomano; and Angro-Mainyus's host consisted of, aside from an additional five major evil lords similar to Akomano, a number of corps com-manders named Destruction, Deceit, Rapine and Poverty.

Man, created by Ahura-Mazda as part of his cosmic scheme, was obliged to join in the war against Angro-Mainyus on the side of his lord and creator, Ahura-Mazda. He was also to live a life as full of religious observances as the life imposed on the people of Israel by Mosaic law, and later still, as that imposed upon the Christians of early times down to and through the Middle Ages by Catholicism, and later, but with less vigour, by Protestantism.

Thus a devil with a complete hierarchy of Hell—Angro-Mainyus, his princess of Hell, Akomano, Suarva, Indra, Tairic, Zaric and Naonhaitya, and his Drukhs, or captains, and beneath them the separate legions of demon-specialists—came into being in the Iranian, Zoroastrian, non-idolatrous religious system that lent itself quite admirably to the needs of later-day theological inno-vators. Nor did they neglect using it, but only in outline form, substituting different, appropriate names, changing whatever needed altering to fit different times and requirements, but maintaining in general a comparable basis.

The Zoroastrians had a Hades, the usual dark and gloomy place of torment and damnation, presided over by Angro-Mainyus and his horde of demons and devils. The idea of Hell as a standardized place of punishment was well fixed in men's minds by the time of the Iranians and Persians. Also, the eternal dualism, good versus evil—go(o)d versus (d)evil—was equally and as unshakably fixed. All the systems differed, naturally, but the devil's image varied least of all, as these ancient theologies borrowed from one another.

The early Indians, for example, enjoyed an extensive polytheism not unlike that of Babylon, Egypt and Assyria, but without the tendency towards monotheism occasionally encountered in those other faiths. The Sanskritic Indians, until the epoch of the Vedic poets passed, and beginning with no more than thirty-three gods, eventually had a pantheon of 3,339 gods!

But the image of their Hell and their devil was almost interchangeable with the Lord of Evil and his realm as known in the other early theologies—although less was said of both, because the Sanskritic Indians were more philosophical about sin, which they considered an inevitable and excusable human weakness. Their sense of guilt was slight, they felt small compulsion towards such things as repentance, improvement of character, or the strength to resist temptation. When they prayed it was rarely for exaltation of the soul, but was instead for more temporal rewards such as food, health, strength, personal happiness, safety from enemies, and wealth.

They were not—not initially at any rate—concerned with an after-life, which fairly well limited the scope of their devil. The Rig-Veda appeared to rather plaintively hope that there might be a future happiness, a serene variety of immortality. It also evidently put a price on salvation: "He who gives alms goes to the highest place in Heaven; he goes to the gods," and would cast into the pit those who offered no sacrifice.

It took a long time for the Sanskritic Indians to evolve towards the popular monotheism. Much change was encountered, but their image of the devil and their concept of Hell changed least of all.

In comparison to the Sanskritic Indians, the ancient Phoenicians scarcely had any pantheon at all. The total number of their gods was no more than twenty, and, interestingly, the major Phoenician gods turned up generations later as Christianity's devils. At least the names were identical. Baal, Ashtoreth (Astoroth), Melkarth, Moloch, Adonis, Dagon, Hadad, Baaltis, Eshmun, Onca, Sadyk, *et cetera*. Actually, 'Baal' signified a local deity of high order and each Phoenician community had its Baal or divine 'lord'. For example at Beirut the Baal was Eshnun and at Tyre the Baal was Melkarth. A particular Phoenician deity was a fly, called a 'zebub'. Thus the name of the fly god was Baal Zebub, cognate to Beelzebub.

The Phoenicians brought the first alphabet to Europe, established Carthage, gave the Greeks their first concepts of art, were the master merchants and seamen of the Aegean world, discovered the westermost Mediterranean and Atlantic Oceans, colonized the far distant Atlantic coast of Spain, and yet evolved only a rather poor theology of their own, borrowing greatly from the religions of their neighbours, even to the point of accepting the concept of Hell, and Satan's image, as evolved by people to whom in many ways the Phoenicians were vastly superior.

Unlike the Etruscans, previously mentioned, who arrived as colonists in early Italy, and whose most pervading principle was theology, the Phoenicians, while not remiss, appeared to be far more concerned with trade, with commerce, with a flourishing, vigorous pragmatism than with a very concerted or complex theology.

The Etruscan devil previously mentioned—a horrible image, hideous, half-man, half-beast, called Charun—was undoubtedly the forerunner of Christianity's Satan. It may also be presumed that the Etruscan concept of Charun's legion of evil demons was a handy forerunner of the Christian concept of a Hell inhabited by many demons and furies, the first and best such hierarchy to appear in mainland Europe, and the hierarchy which was destined to survive, as devils always have, long after the more benevolent gods had disappeared.

The ancient Greeks also had a complex theology; nowhere, not even in the Roman pantheon, was there ever such a multitudinous polytheism. The Sanskritic Indians, with more than 3,000 deities, ran far behind the aggregate of quasi-human or ultra-human personages of ancient Greece, ranging from heroes, nymphs, demons, genii, to the spirits inhabiting the mountains, rivers, villages, even Greek cattle and canines. Oreads lived in the forests in droves; springs and waterfalls had naiads, every oak tree had a resident spirit, a dryad.

There were at least five definite orders, or classes, of Greek dieties. Zeus was *the* god, father of the Gods, the God of gods. Zeus and Olympus, residence of the gods, were at the apex of the Hellenic theology, but the brother of Zeus, named Hades (or Aidoneus) was the lord of the underworld, co-equal with Zeus in most ways, and of all the vast array of Greek gods, Hades was the least defined, unless that distinction went to his wife, Persephone, queen of the dead, who was chaste, severe, awful in wrath and terrible in vengeance, but not cruel.

Hades was *"magni nominis umbra"*, the shadow of a great name. He was obscure and solemn, but for two reasons was never very aptly defined by the Greeks. The foremost reason was because he ruled the nether world and the Greek theology was infinitely more preoccupied with events and personages in the upper world of Olympus. The second reason was that Hellenes held to a pleasant, joyous, light and gossipy kind of theology, and were neither much troubled by a sense of sin nor very worried about their after-life prospects. They reverenced Hades as a deity, but did not particularly fear or respect him.

They did not in fact respect most of their gods, but they were careful and prudent in their religious observances. When a Greek made a vow, perhaps in exchange for a swift recovery from illness, he was scrupulous in his discharge of it.

The ancient Hellenes attributed to their nether world a good bit of discomfort, and the image of their underworld king was consistent with similar images among all ancient people. However, unlike some, such as the Etruscans, the Greeks did not create an elaborate realm of eternal gloom dominated by an unrelentingly hideous and sadistic Devil who was devoted to the downfall of mankind.

According to Plato, the average Greek had no deep sense of guilt, and most of the crimes committed had analogies in the crimes committed by the gods, who were thus understanding. An appropriate offering would usually placate them and reinstate the citizen of Greece in good grace.

The early Romans, unlike the early Hellenes, had only a few principal divinities. They were Olympic gods with Latin names:

Jupiter, Juno, Mars, Minerva, Neptune, Vesta, Apollo, Venus, Ceres, Bellona, Saturnus, Ops, Hercules, Diana, Mercurius and Bacchus.

The Roman pantheon was largely borrowed, most of the gods deriving from Sabine, Greek or Latin sources. Nor did the Romans treat their gods as lightly as did the Greeks, even though their secondary deities were almost as numerous, and as vulnerable as were the Greek deities.

But, analogous with Phoenician worship, Roman religion was not in accord with Roman politics and empirical ambition, and it suffered accordingly, ultimately substituting ritualism for piety, and offering hypocrisy in the place of religious observance. Lucretius declared that religion was the curse of the human race, and in his own time and place he was correct, for the religion of Rome, grafted on to a way of life that was alien to borrowed gods, had little effect on the daily life of Romans.

The Devil's image in Rome was not very different from that of many Roman gods, and his demons, the fauns of Rome, were similar to the satyrs of Greece.

By the time in history when the Roman Empire was dominant, the Devil as a personage had a rather fixed and static image. Only when—as with the Romans and the Sanskritic Indians—there was no great conviction concerning salvation, rebirth or an elevating after-life, did the devil's image become unimportant, or at least relatively unimportant.

Nonetheless, the image, borrowed elsewhere and already an ancient amalgam by the time the Romans adopted it, was solidly based and unalterably fixed. The Roman lower classes knew about Hell and its overlord, but like the upper class Romans, they preferred to believe that gods punished men and nations. Their basis for such a belief was elemental; some men fell ill and wasted, and other men did not. Some nations lost vigour, other nations flourished. The visible proof of vindictive gods lay on every hand, and as long as people felt that gods could be malevolent and treacherous, their feelings toward the Devil could be rather sanguine.

The people who gave Rome such trouble as colonials, the Hebrews, after 400 years of captivity in Egypt, could scarcely have avoided being influenced by the Egyptian polytheism. As the

Egyptians worshipped the bulls of Apis, so did the Jews seek to exalt golden calves in the wilderness. As the Egyptians exalted priests, the Hebrews made their priests national and tribal leaders. As the Egyptians loathed swine, the ancient Jews abhorred pork.

In their early years the Hebrews encountered all the great theologies. From the Persians they learned about an individual Lord of Evil, a personal and real devil. He came into their theology already formed; all that was required of the Jews was that they adapt his image to their own time and place. They could do this easily since in ancient times they had believed in good and wicked immortals, much as did the later Romans. It was very simple, then, to accord the historic devil a place in the Hebrew theology.

From there, since the latter-day monotheism that exalted Yahweh as the supreme god, required a contending counterpart, the Devil, as a Hebrew extenuation of the age-old struggle between good and evil—the ancient dualism—assumed his fixed place. Also, because Yahweh was a jealous god, and because the Satan of the Hebrews could best spite the traditional foes of Israel, it was later suggested that Satan was in fact a great god of the heathen heretics. Priapus, for example, the son of Aphrodite (the Roman god Mutunus), notorious for sexual orgies performed in his honour, was cast in the roll of a terrible demon by the Hebrews, eventually being termed King of Hell.

Of course other pagan deities also earned this designation including the great god Zeus. But in the early stages the Devil as Satan was not considered a prominent demon. In fact he is scarcely mentioned in the Old Testament, except, as in the Book of Job, where he is mentioned as being an angel whose duty was to patrol the world and report human sins to God. Otherwise his image is shadowy, although he was not a very commendable personage. So he arrived in Hebrew theology as he similarly arrived in earlier —and later—religions, already established as a personification of evil in all its recognizable forms. His diabolism hinged upon what each faith believed most devoutly in, i.e., the Greeks acknowledged his existence but did not particularly dread him because their theology put no premium on heavenly blackmail, while the Hebrews feared him and made him nearly as formidable as their Yahweh, because their faith required a strong incentive to keep an originally idolatrous people pure in their latter-day monotheism. Gnostics, on the other hand, after the advent of Christianity, believed that the Hebrew Jehovah was the Devil; by the admission of his followers He had created earth, and the Gnostics held that the world of man's five senses was an epitome of evil, to be scorned and renounced.

Regardless of his origin, of his function, of his appearance—and they all differed in different epochs—the Devil's image was black and totally evil. He came into the consciousness of man as malevolent, and that is the image of him that has persevered ever since. Many gods have come, and gone, but the King of Hell not only remained, he did so almost unscathed.

FIVE

The Devil's Diversity

With nothing more tangible than *hope*, rational man has lived with an enduring scepticism respecting an after-life, his conviction little changed since prehistoric times. Of *theories* there has been an unending procession; of *proof* one way or another there has been none, and there remains none. Despite many elaborate religions, and regardless of how powerful, engulfing and militant these have been, in general mankind has never been convinced death was not complete finality.

All man has ever known, and all he still knows of death is that flowers wilt, trees disintegrate; everything that was upright in life falls down in death, and what is not buried *in* the earth is ultimately absorbed *by* the earth.

Death has always been *assumed* to be more dolorous than life, thus Hades, at least for those who were to be eternally banished, was a cruel place, and the lord of Hell, whatever he may have been elsewhere, was a relentlessly cruel lord.

Often, he was thought to have once been an archangel, a god; in fact, as in the case of Zeus, he was thought at one time to have been *the* god.

Hades, which was originally a designation, or personification, of the tomb, later became an individual, a god or lord of that Other Place. Still later, Hades lost his individuality as travel and ideological miscegenation flourished, crossing seas, mountains, forests and steppes; he again became a *place*, the underworld Hell.

In Icelandic the word *helja* meant to hide. To be dead was to be hidden, to be gone forever. There was an Icelandic goddess, Hel, who was, like Hades, first the designation for a *place* (but unlike most early concepts of that Other Place, the Icelandic underworld was frigid, not hot). Then the designation was changed and Hel became the queen of the dead, only to be transformed at a later date to a place again. Hel became the destination of the soul which, after the body was put into the earth, kept going straight down into Hell.

Hell, Sheol, Tartarus, Hades, the Valley of the Shadow of Death, by whatever name, because it was associated with an unknown and presumed darkness, was associated with the Greek *Thanatos*, death, with all the myth and legend of a dark, inner earth that absorbed the dead, whether flower or tree or ambulatory human being. And because Hell was the personification of total finality, of which no one actually knew anything at all, it had to be a fearful place, and its ruler had to be the arch enemy of all life. "The senseless dead," Homer said of Hell's inhabitants, "the simulacra of mortals." And Isaiah (xxxviii, 18) said: "For the grave cannot praise thee, death cannot celebrate thee: they that go down into the pit cannot hope for thy truth."

Zeus, who was, like Odin of the Teutons, a mighty hunter, was also an admirer of women. Of his many wives—who were actually symbols like Metis, who was the power of Thought, and Themis, who was Law—all were creative; and even when mighty Zeus was sent to Hell, to join the legend of evil Charun and become the Satan of Christianity, he took with him his power, his lusts, and his whims.

As Charun was "a squalid and hideous old man with flaming eyes and savage aspect . . . the ears and often the tusks of a brute", Zeus came to Hell noted among Christians as a powerful and lecherous demon. Usually, as with the Etruscan overlord of Hades, Mantus, as well as Charun, Satan had wings. Baal, or Baal Zebub of Phoenicia, being a fly, had wings. Dionysos, whose symbol was a goat, was another pagan god termed a demon by Christianity. Like Pan the satyr, Dionysos was alleged to have cloven hooves. The mysteries of Isis in ancient Egypt were concerned with a goat, thus the idea of the Prince of Darkness possessing wings and cloven hooves evolved without difficulty, and the Devil's diversity began to assume a form, an enduring image that later theologies such as Christianity sustained.

Perhaps because death was the antithesis of life, and the overriding consideration from earliest times was propagation, natural human reaction in the face of death was defiance in the form of generation and regeneration. If death, the greatest threat of all, hovered in the shadows, an eternal enemy of life and living things, then, quite reasonably, frail and vulnerable, but resolute living man had of necessity to neutralize the peril as best he could.

He did it through phallicism. The magician's wand, the priest's mitre, the fetishist's erect snake, were symbols of man's generative organ, his phallus, his only means for circumventing the purpose, if not the individuality, of death. A king's sceptre was a phallic symbol. The caduceus, modern medicine's symbol, two serpents entwined in an embrace about an upright phallus, is symbolic of regenerative life. Church spires are phallic symbols.

In early times tombstones, called 'matzevoth' in the Bible, were round and erect, their meaning unmistakably phallic. If death conquered the person lying below, each matzevoth above proved that generation was invincible above. Christians and Jews could, and often did, destroy the symbols of pagan theologies, and yet they too worshipped at upright, round stone altars, as implacable as the pagans ever were in their reverence of the divine principle of generation.

Satan himself, like the obscene idol Priapus, was endowed with an outsized lust. During Christianity's apex he was epitomized as a violently sexual entity. It was recorded any number of times that he would appear among mortals, at witches' sabbats and elsewhere, with an enormous erection, and copulate with as many as 100 women in one night. In this way even the symbol of death himself was forced to represent the purpose of life, and although it was inevitable that this aspect of Satanism became debased to a restrictive lewdness, copulation between demons and mortals for the simple sake of intercourse, the basic idea was never lost sight of. That was, fundamentally, that Charun, Zeus, Baal Zebub, Satan, by all his earliest names, had been coerced into performing the function that was in opposition to what he stood for—death, which was destruction.

The original maypole was a phallic symbol. The bull as well as the goat was symbolic because of the known carnal capacity each possessed. Christianity's image of Satan with a bull's horns, and a cloven hoof, or two cloven hooves, left Satan endowed with the symbols of human triumph through reproduction. His tail, held erect and in form similar to a serpent, was additional symbolism.

The Devil's diversity did not crystelize until after the Christian advent for most of the Western world, but when it eventually did assume fixed form, Satan became an excellent amalgam of the ancient ideas. Pan and his cohorts the satyrs—the fauns of Rome —like Dionysos, and of course Priapus, were embodiments of the sexuality deriving from historic times, passed on to Satan and his cherubim, sylphs and undines, so that by the period of Christianity's advent, the sexuality as well as all the forms and images were ready at hand to populate Hell, Satan's dark and terrible realm, exactly as Satan's image was also formed and fixed.

But this crystelization of the Devil's diversity did not occur at once. For one thing there were too many eligible pagan gods; for another, no one specific god or demon possessed all the evil attributes Christians wished for in their lord of Hell. But perhaps the main reason the Bible was vague about Satan as an individual was that at the time of its initial compilation there was no unanimity of opinion concerning Satan as an entity.

Reference to the Devil as representative of evil is made in many biblical passages, both in the Old and New Testaments, yet there is no full account in any one place, and Scriptural revelations are so vague that a composite emerges only when all the innuendos between Genesis and Apocalypse are combined.

Understandably, Christianity in its youth was not at all as it became in its middle age. Not until the fourth Latern Council in fact did Satan or evil demons achieve particularity. Prior to that time the genesis of Satan was still fulminating. It was much simpler to populate Hell. All the old pagan gods, most of whom were lesser deities in any case, could be collectively swept downward to become Christianity's imps and demons; but fleshing-out a particular chief devil was difficult and it took time, exactly as it also took time to create a creditable hierarchy, both of Heaven *and* of Hell.

The Roman god Bacchus, like the Indian deity Siva, had as his symbol an erect phallus. Bacchus, also called Liber, was responsible, each March, for the festival of Liberalia, which was to symbolize the regeneration of nature after the long somnolence of winter. Wine was drunk and frenzied dancing ended in sexual orgies that shocked the Christians. Romans saw nothing obscene in any of this; its purpose was to celebrate the re-emergence of nature's profuse generative activity. Romans merely encouraged that return of Nature's power by emulating it. But Christianity seized upon the Bacchanalias as an epitome of degradation; to their Satan was attributed this additional sexual depravity, although in fact he did not need it, having already inherited an adequate amount from Osiris, Zeus, Pan, all the other and older pagan gods, whose greatest, most venerated power lay in their control of a divine life-principle.

Christianity's Satan began to be recognizable, finally. He was incredibly amoral. He was half-man, half-beast. He was God's tireless foe, as well as man's eternal temptor and destroyer. As the epitome of all evil he was, like most other devils, representative of the invincible aspect of all duality. God could not conquer him, but neither, allegedly, could he conquer God.

He was King of Hell. Subordinate to him were legions of inferior but equally as tireless devils, each a member of some specific division within the hierarchy of Hell. He never rested and could only be propitiated by human debasement, sexual or otherwise.

His power was great; in many cases it was as great as the power of Christianity's God. In this, as in almost all else, Christianity's Satan did not differ at all from the pagan Lords of Darkness. He survived countless aeons scarcely changed and came into the Christian monotheism old and vastly subtle, leaving behind the pagan pantheons. But all those other gods against whom he had contended for so many earlier millennia, now were his slaves. He had conquered and, unless the concept of Hell changes entirely— there is no reason for it to do so any more in the future than there was in the past—Satan probably will conquer Christianity's God too, when, in another historic epoch the Yahweh of Judaism, which is the Lord God of Christianity, will yield to the next ensuing enlightenment—serving, or convenience-serving, concept of God.

Thus Satan's diversity, presently fixed in concept and image, enjoyed one notable—and significant—aspect. It was eternal, more so than that of all previous deities; and those who created the acceptable amalgam also made apparent the fact that while God, in order to endure, must be amenable to constant change, constant renewal, Satan as an epitome of evil could rely forever on a superior seniority.

The Gate of Hell, one of William Blake's illustrations for Dante's
Inferno

(left) A fifteenth-century drawing of 'The Prince of Darkness'. *(below)* A medieval caricature of the Satanic goat

Toned-down latter-day Christianity characterized Satan with a trident, with cloven hooves it chose not to explain, and with horns and a tail it further preferred not to discuss, until Satan's mere ugliness was supposed to inspire fear and revulsion. But Satan's sexuality, the erect phallus, borrowed from ancient pagans, was actually his symbol, as it always was, but not in the same sense as with Bacchus and Pan and the other deities of generation; Satan's phallus represented triumph over death, not especially the saving fecundity of nature. He was cursed by man to carry these symbols wherever he went. Even as he raked in souls he was compelled to mock himself by appearing in the image of *life*-death.

He came, finally, to the Christian pantheon, with its angels and archangels who could also be prayed to, as he had come to all those other pantheons; the Olympus of the great gods of other times became Christianity's Heaven. Zeus had been replaced by Jehovah, by a different God, but most of all else was familiar. He even witnessed the death of another deity—Jesus—as he had witnessed similar deaths before, when the gods Apollo, Balder, Heracles, and the many vulnerable gods of Hellas, also died.

New forms were suited to a different time, and in due course a different ecology, an altered etymology; but in substance, even in concept and ritual, there was very little basic change. The Hebrews and the Christians evolved little that was original, thus Satan could adjust without difficulty.

The Jewish aversion to pork, shared by Mohammedans, arose from the Egyptian aversion. For as long as the Jews were captive they observed the Egyptian hatred of swine. Of all Egyptians only swineherds were not allowed to worship in the temples. When Israel's people were yielded up out of Egypt they brought the Egyptian aversion with them. Nothing much was new.

When Christianity defined Hell, it was the same place pagans had defined, with some enhancement. When Christians confirmed Satan he was recognizable. The flow of theological surmise evolved with more originality up to the eras of Yahweh and Jehova than it did afterwards, and Satan suffered least of all.

All the characteristics of earlier devils were included—along with whatever additions were requisite, and they were negligible—to complete a consolidation of all the tenuous disparities. Satan assumed an image that was to last almost 2,000 years; his most

D

serious jeopardy arrived only when Christianity made him ludicrous, for then he was injured as never before, by neglect—not
by ridicule or, as with the Greeks, a polite lip-service—but
by candid and dispassionate neglect. Devils, like gods, have
never been able to survive being ignored; in only this one respect
are they both vulnerable.

SIX

Christianity's Satan

The diversity of Satan was vague in I Samuel, xvi, 14, and the "lying spirit" of I Kings, xxii, 22 was an impersonal metaphor. In the post-exilic notations, as in Job, Satan assumed a recognizable form, and, while he was an adversary and antagonist, different in principle from Jehovah, yet he appeared among the sons of God (Job, ii, 1).

His duty was to tempt men, and in this guise he could be said to have been a personification of literal and unequivocal justice— he would not be bribed or diverted, only qualified good was acceptable to him.

In this form he was acceptable to the latter-day monotheism of the Hebrews, but the ultimate notion of Satan as God's rival found in the Apocrypha, and assumed in the New Testament, was undoubtedly a result of influential Persian theological thought on the Hebrews. The Asmodeus of Tobit, iii, is an equivalent to Satan, an evil entity, while in Wisdom, ii, 24, he is equalled with the serpent of Genesis, iii. In Baruch serpent gods are termed demons, and finally, in the Secrets of Enoch, Satanail is expelled from Heaven.

The Book of Enoch offered an incomplete hierarchy of Hell, from Satan as king through the demons who were fallen angels, the latter, not originally of evil nature, sharing this distinction with Satan before his fall.

From this genesis, then, evolved the source of a personal devil who both tempted and punished those who succumbed to evil, in the Talmudic and Christian theologies. He was an amalgam of pagan myth and later-day concept, formed to fit, not necessarily new, but certainly altered, cosmogonies.

The gospels came forth to ultimately reveal a kingdom of evil ruled by Satan, also known as Beelzebub, the lord of demons (Matthew, xii, 24), to whom Jesus alleged physical and moral wickedness (Luke, xiii, 16; Mark, iv, 15).

The Apostle Paul contended that there were powers, dominions, and principalities of evil, and that Satan, or Belial, as their overlord, as the original cause of earthy ills, was the chief seducer of souls.

In the Apocalypse the struggle between good and evil paralleled most of the ancient pagan conceptions of this eternal duality, and in the second century the death of Jesus was held by many churchmen to be the ransom that had to be paid to cause Satan to withdraw.

St. Augustine, among others, saw Satan's kingdom as sharing the world with God's kingdom, and during the Middle Ages theologians and laymen came very close to professing an analogy that was no different from much earlier pagan superstition. When later theologians would have banished Satan as a sure way to resolve the implications of a possible triumph of evil, they were frustrated by Jesus himself, who apparently accepted the existence, and individuality, of Satan.

The evil entity, Satan, came close to following the example of Hades and Hel, when, from a wicked physical demon, he became also a variety of abstract moral evil. Monotheism, Hebrew and Christian—paralleling Zoroastrianism which cast Ahriman as the evil antagonist to Ahura-Mazda—pitted Satan the evil entity against Jahveh (Jehovah), thus preventing Satan's individuality from degenerating into a *place*. But by the era of Christian advent monotheism had quite supplanted ancient polytheism; the pantheons still existed—millions of evangelized pagans continued secretly to pay homage to the old gods—but monotheism, the result of progressive enlightenment, was achieving an enduring prominence, and monotheism included monodemonism. Thus Satan the composite retained his individuality and a Christian nexus was born; demonology, the science of religion which dealt with the existence and nature of a supposed realm of spirits possessing powers of evil over men.

It was this science that broadened the base of Hell and widened its scope. Satan, already adequately entitled, acquired additional names. In Matthew (xxv, 41) he was "the devil and his angels".

He was also Lucifer, the name patristic writers gave him before his fall, as well as the Hebrew *satan* and the Greek *satanas*, meaning God's adversary, a popular version of which was adopted by Christ at the temptation on the mount: "Get thee behind me, *Satan*." (Luke, iv, 8). In Revelation (xii, 9) he was "the great dragon . . . that old serpent, called the Devil, and *Satan* . . . cast out into the earth, and his angels . . . with him."

The designation *Devil*, derived from the Greek *diabalos*, meant originally a traducer, an accuser, but the original Greek *satanas*, as God's enemy, was not necessarily also man's enemy.

Devils were demons, imps. In its original Greek form, *daemon*, this word designated friendly, guardian spirits; but the Greek Septuagint used the term demon in reference to evil or vengeful idols (Hebrew: *schedim*) and in this form it passed through a latinised interpretation and became the designation for evil spirits, while devils (not capitalized except in reference to *the* Devil, Satan) of Hell, also known as imps *et cetera*, while doing Satan's work, were not *the* Devil, even when they impersonated him.

It did not help any when latter-day demonologists such as the Englishman, Wycliffe, referred to devils as *fiends*, an old Anglo-Saxon word meaning enemy.

Nor did it dissipate the confusion when the names of the old pagan gods were used; thus Asmodeus the old time deity became, in the Book of Tobit, the demon lover of the fair Sara, and ancient Phoenicia's god Baal Zebub became Beelzebub "the chief of devils" (Luke, xi, 15). Behemoth, Belial, Dagon, Leviathan, used almost indiscriminately, came eventually to designate not Satan, but his princes of Hell, and all were associated in earlier times with loftier, if pagan, entities, as later, they were also used to designate Satan.

The Council of Toledo, in A.D. 447, legalized the Devil, who by then had been rather well established in the Christian theology. Subsequently *he* changed hardly at all, but his demons changed, or at least they stood revealed in different ways, although it is possible they were always as subsequent revelations depicted them, and mankind had not known it.

For churchmen the confusing pantheon of Hell was not only very real, it was also reasonable, but churchmen lived in their own, separate world. The secular world of warfare, famine, natural calamities and political upheaval had little time for monasticism; the average Christian from the Advent onward was more immediately concerned with simple survival. He accepted Hell's concept as defined by theologians, verbatim, whether he was lord, peasant, or king. When it was said that devils frequently changed their shape "taking the forms of women, wild beasts, creeping things, gigantic bodies and troops of soldiers", he accepted this as consistent with that which was subtly, slyly, evil. Devils assumed "the appearance of monks, and feigned the speech of holy men".

In the *Life of St. Anthony* it was noted that devils often appeared after first creating a fearful din, a terrifying commotion. They were also capable, as was noted in the *Life of St. Hilary*, of passing through locked doors, and frequently were known to be present, although invisible, by their dreadful stench. St. Hilary, so it was averred, got to know which devil was present by the smell.

Also, said learned Christian theologians, devils, including Satan, did not necessarily create a body for themselves out of air, but took possession of human or animal bodies among living creatures. Thus it was that the devil, Legion (Mark, v), inhabited the Gaderene swine; and in medieval times it was not only legal, but very desirable to torture to death and burn at the stake hundreds of thousands of human beings accused of being possessed.

As Mara, Buddhism's Devil, Satan was recognizable among Christian churchmen; so was Mephistopheles ("not loving of light") the demon Dr. Johann Faustus allegedly brought forth during the great spiritual upheaval known as the Reformation, at which time even Doctor Faustus's name became associated with this dreaded being, Faust.

Satan's power for evil was limitless. Theologians had the millennial precepts to draw from. They could, and did, controvert to Christianity's use all the grisly legends of paganism's ingenuity. The fall was not an original concept; throughout pre-Christian centuries the casting out of devils was common to most theologies. The Christian concept was solemnly confirmed: "I beheld Satan as lightning fall from Heaven" (Luke, x, 18).

But all this led only to a question: what, specifically, led Satan to commit his great crime; how could an angel, who was not possessed of the weaknesses of mortal flesh, greed, envy, hatred, lust, but whose angelic nature was totally pure, do an evil thing?

The answer (Isaiah, xiv, 13) had to do with Satan's desire for equality with God—envy—and again the corollary was found in any one of paganism's myths, except that whereas most pagan deities, modelled after mortal men, were liable to be envious, Christianity's angels were too powerfully and perfectly pure to know such baseness. Thus when Christianity borrowed the concept of the Fall, having created also such pure immortals, there was an embarrassing discrepancy, and it was never satisfactorily resolved, although Churchmen by the score rushed to the breach, either unmindful or ignorant of a fact of basic mortal existence: that no man is less to be trusted than when he seeks to establish an alibi.

But the Devil existed; neither churchman or layman dared raise the doubt. Subsequent to the Fall his image (as in the Eliphas Levi drawing) changed very little: he had Pan's feet, Charun's disposition, Priapus's genitals—although discreetly robed in later times—Zeus's thunder, Moloch's craft, Ahriman's maliciousness, and the tireless enthusiasm for evil of Seth and Mara, plus the gloom and cruelty, the energetic sadism as well, of all earlier Lords of Darkness.

In form he could appear human (the Catholics said he sired Martin Luther by deceiving Luther's mother) or he could appear as a rank goat, but generally he was depicted, at the very least, with one cloven hoof, horns, a phallic tail, usually with a hairy and physically powerful body. In the Garden of Eden one of his princes, Asmodeus, appeared as the unctiously ingratiating viper and seduced Eve, but when Satan went forth, for whatever purpose —and he was ever mindful of opportunities for ravishing mortal women—he was always motivated by his sole obsession: defiance of God and the debasement of man who was made in the likeness of God and God's son. Thus he was almost invariably recognizable, if not at the moment of appearance, certainly afterwards when his sly malevolence stood revealed.

Everlastingly arrayed with his hosts in warfare against God and man, after the first triumph—in the garden—his strength grew immeasurably. As director of all elements of evil his subtlety was endless; he had triumphed over two-thirds of mankind, according to divine authority, in ways mankind scarcely recognized. Through persecution of the enlightened, for example, making their earthly existence a living Hell. He triumphed over the indifferent and irreligious by giving them ease and comfort and wealth. Rich men *belonged* to Satan. Over the very ignorant he triumphed through superstition, fanaticism, and heresy.

In the words of Father W. H. Kent, O.S.C., "It would be bad enough if all these forces were acting apart and without any definite purpose, but the perils of the situation are incalculably increased when all may be organized and directed by [Satan's] vigilant and hostile intelligences. It is this that makes the Apostle, though he well knew the perils of the world and the weakness of the flesh, lay special stress on the greater dangers that come from the assaults of these mighty spirits of evil in whom he recognized our real and most formidable foes—'Put you on the armour of God, that you may be able to stand against the deceits of the devil. . . .' "

In the Teutonic Eddas Loki, the deity of funeral pyres, was a malevolent spirit who possessed two wives, Asgard and a giantess named Angraboda. Of the wives of Zeus several have been previously mentioned, while the great German god, Odihinn (Wuotan), who also degenerated into an embodiment of Satan, had his 'shield maidens', his Valkyriur.

The Etruscan lord of Hell, Mantus, had a queen, previously noted, named Mania. Throughout the ancient theologies wives and consorts of devils were common. When Dr. Faustus attended a meeting of the notables of Hell he was attracted to, and was warned against, a beautiful demon named Lilith, called Satan's consort, known as Queen of the Succubi, or female demons, and also categorized as the First Lady of Hell. She was a direct importation into Christianity from the Hebrew theology, that defined her as the consort of a devil named Samael.

In Isaiah, xxxiv, 14, Lilith is alluded to. In the Latin Vulgate Lilith is rendered "Lamia", meaning simply an evil spirit in female form—a witch—but the English translation renders the name into "screech-owl", rather thoroughly misinterpreting it entirely.

Lilith was an ancient demon, borrowed by the Hebrews from paganism; and when the rabbins who adopted her were required to explain who she was, they proclaimed her as Adam's first wife. Eve was Adam's second wife. For proof they offered the first chapter of Genesis where it said God created a human pair. That, then, would be Adam and Lilith. But in the second chapter of Genesis, God had Adam fall into a deep sleep and fashioned a woman, Eve, out of one of Adam's ribs.

These events, then, were two separate and distinct occurrences. Originally, it was alleged that God created man and woman, joined as one back to back. "Male and female He created them, and called their name Adam." They quarrelled constantly until Lilith pronounced the ineffable name, a cabbalistic charm ever after, acquired wings along with separation, and flew away.

Adam in distress and loneliness cried out and the Lord sent three angels to order her back to Eden. Lilith refused to obey. The Lord then sent a warning: unless she returned all her children would die in infancy. In her despair Lilith contemplated suicide and the compassionate angels, taking pity, offered a solution: Lilith should have power over all children unto their eighth day of life, which was thought to somewhat mitigate the curse.

In return Lilith promised never to harm babies under the particular care of the three angels. For centuries Jews hung a charm, called a *camea* around the necks of newborn babies, in it was written the names of the three angels. Otherwise the high death-rate of babies during early biblical times was attributed to Lilith, the cursed first wife of Adam, the consort of Satan.

While Lilith was in her great distress she encouraged a demon namer Samuel, and became his companion. In Christian theology there was no marriage, which was a holy estate, a sacrament, and could not be performed beyond the influence of the church. Be that as it was, Lilith went to Hell with Samael, becoming by the Middle Ages Queen of the Succubi.

Lilith was a nymphomaniac: whether or not she was one in her pagan form, she certainly evolved into one by the time she had passed into the Christian theology. She frequently appeared among mortals, seducing men and afterwards strangling them with her long hair. This hair was, during her Hebrew sojourn, dark, but Christianity changed the colour to golden. Many mortals and demons, including Dr. Faustus, were as enthralled by Lilith's beautiful hair as by her other handsome attributes.

But Lilith's disposition, which made her an outcast from Eden, did not change in Hell, where her capacity for sexual gratification made her especially well-suited to teach, inform, encourage, and even to guide, the succubi, the lewd female demons, in their eternal conquests among men. But Lilith as Queen of Hell was suited also to the position of Satan's inamorata, even though in the Christian pantheon of Hell latter-day chroniclers had begun to ignore her even before the Middle Ages, and by the Reformation she had almost passed from the scene, perhaps because it was more creditable, as well as more suitable to the theme of everlasting temptation, for Satan to seduce mortal women.

Robert, son of a Duchess of Normandy, was the product of such a union, as was Martin Luther. Angela, Lady of Labarthe, tortured and put to the stake in the year 1275 at age 65, gave herself to Satan, and the result was an appalling monster with a wolf's head and his father's tail. Merlin, the incomparable magician, was sired by Satan out of a pious maiden who protected herself against the Devil's lascivious insinuations by constantly crossing herself, but one night she forgot and in due course, a matter of three-quarters of a year, she gave birth to a boy-child. Satan bequeathed to his progeny, who was born normal in appearance, a knowledge of the past, and the Lord, eager to win Satan's son to the cause of righteousness, gave young Merlin a knowledge of the future, and thus he became so famous as a magician and soothsayer that his name to this day is synonymous with miracles.

Satan as King of Hell became a most durable transplant, not only because of his untiring zeal in the cause of evil, but also because according to many early theologians, aside from siring Merlin, Martin Luther, and Robert of Normandy, he also fathered the entire population of the island of Cyprus, and moreover, as the organizer of the hierarchy of Hell, he displayed a genius never equalled on earth, and rarely, if ever, in Heaven.

SEVEN

The Hierarchy of Hell

A rather comprehensive list of devils, the hierarchy to which each belonged, as well as their functions, was compiled by Father Sebastian Michaelis, a noted exorcist, in his *Admirable History* published in 1612. His source was none other than Balberith, Prince of Cherubim, First Hierarchy of Hell, whom Father Michaelis exorcized from a nun, Sister Madeleine de Demandolx de la Palud of Aix-en-Provence, France, in 1610, when Father Michaelis was Grand Inquisitor of Avignon.

But the *Testament of Solomon*, which preceded the Michaelis account by some 1500 years, gives an account of Hell's hierarchy dating from earliest times, and, like the Michaelis recitation, had as its source a devil, this one named Ornias, a leach-devil, or vampire-demon.

Ornias sucked so much blood from one of Solomon's slaves that Solomon called upon God for help. The angel Raphael appeared, bringing to Solomon a magic ring. With this charm Solomon was able to subdue and command all demons. Beginning with Ornias, Solomon summoned, among others, fifteen devils of rank, compelled each to identify himself, his hierarchy, his functions, and to also name the angel of God who could thwart his evil.

After each interrogation Solomon put the devils to work at the Temple or else he had them imprisoned so they could do no more harm.

But the *Testament* also listed more than fifty demons from whom it was possible to obtain material benefits—which derived from infernal power, however, and were therefore not to be considered lightly—as well as the thirty-six *decani*, spirits of the Zodiac, who have an evil association with the different parts of the human body (and seemed to derive almost unaltered from ancient Chaldean disease-demons), so there was a mixed blessing to be found in Solomon's *Testament*. The demons and *decani* not only obligingly explained themselves, they also gave Solomon the key to each curse by naming the angel whose intercession counteracted their evil.

Solomon's *Testament* was incomplete; every categorized hierarchy of Hell is incomplete. No sooner is one evolved than fresh revelations add to it, shuffle the demons from category to category, broaden the foundation and increase the number of devils, or, simply because new arrivals in Hell, hourly and daily, make new names and fresh assignments mandatory and inevitable, there can never be a complete hierarchy of Hell.

The *Testament of Solomon*, a chief source of information on Hell from A.D. 100 until about A.D. 250 differed in many ways from later works, not only in categorizing demons, but also in alluding to Beelzebub (Beelzeboul) as the first Lord of Hell, which honour belonged to Satan. "Why art thou alone prince of the demons?" asked Solomon, and Beelzebub answered: "Because I alone am left of the angels of Heaven that came down. For I was first angel in the first Heaven . . . and now I control all those who are bowed in Tartarus. . . ."

Actually, Beelzebub was a *prince* of Hell, not its lord, who was Satan, also known at times as Lucifer, but this revelation did not obtain until long after the passing of mighty Solomon, King of Kings, author of *Proverbs* and *Ecclesiastes*, hero of both Talmud and Bible, known in the Koran, great wiseman of the *Arabian Nights* whose age and fall were great when, as a worshipper of rusty gods and as a lover of strange women, the greatest celebrant of ceremonial ritualism of all time went into the shadows having cast his image ahead even 2,000 years. His ring of the pentalpha, brought by the angel Raphael made Solomon, while alive, master of the legions of demons; he needed no other authentication to author his *Testament*, and, incomplete though it became, nevertheless, for two millennia it was a chief reference. From this source arose the subsequent texts—although such authorities as Porphyry (A.D. 233–304) among others chose simply to view spirits as either good or bad, with some mitigations, and to thus avoid the frustrations certain to follow particularizing—but latter-day theologians, pedantic and zealous, went back to the *Testament*, up-dating and enhancing it, or offering various departures until, as time passed, accounts such as that of Sebastian Michaelis, aged Inquisitor of Avignon, confirmed, more or less, the accepted hierarchy, at least in its gradations and in its orders and sub-orders.

By the fourth century the angelic court sponsored by Paul (Collossians, i, 16; Ephesians, i, 21) offered confirmation of the empirical structure of Hell, which was not altered very much afterwards. But the overwhelming array of names, not only of Satan, whose designations became fewer under the Christian aegis, but also of the demons of Hell, multiplied as the authorities on both hell and devils proliferated.

Iamblichus, who died in A.D. 333, worked out a descending hierarchy of spirits beginning with good spirits and concluding with those which were not good, but which were not entirely or consistently evil, either. All were elementals. Proclus (412–84), inheriting from Iamblichus, divided spirits into the five categories. Paracelsus (1493–1541) later proclaimed Proclus's demons ruled water, fire, earth and air, and the nether world, or underworld. These were not all *evil* demons; some could be harmless and even helpful. But usually, these spirits were not considered *devils*, but rather 'daemons', unpleasant and soulless elemental entities.

J. Tritheim offered a hierarchy, a *Liber Officiorum*, in 1575. This listed sixty-nine devils complete with offices and functions giving the names of the kings of the four areas of Hell; North, South, East and West: Amaymon, Goap, Gerson, and Zymymar. The Tritheim *Pseudomanarchia Daemonum* offered names unknown, or at least un-recorded, by the author of Solomon's *Testament*, confirming that by the year 1575 Hell's hierarchy had undergone many changes, and suggesting by this fact that it could very well indeed undergo many more, which it did by the time Father Michaelis compiled his *Admirable History* in 1612.

The Middle Ages saw a diminution of the earlier periods of flux. This constant changing never ceased, but by the seventeenth century Christianity, its stranglehold on the Western world secure, accepted a more or less consistent hierarchy. There were, for example, nine sub-orders of fallen angels (devils), each within

the framework of three exalted orders. The first hierarchy consisted of seraphim, who, in normal form as heavenly angels, had
six wings, and as fallen angels retained this distinction; cherubin,
noted among both heavenly and hellish hosts as possessing wings,
chubby bodies and children's features; and thrones, identifiable
with the seraphim and cherubim, who were simply members,
workers, of the third sub-order of the first hierarchy, and,
like their associates of this hierarchy, corresponded to their
angelic or heavenly counterparts in name, if not in purity and
goodness.

The second hierarchy of Hell consisted of, first, dominions;
secondly, principalities, and thirdly, powers.

The third hierarchy of Hell had as its sub-orders virtues, archangels and angels, each retaining in Hell the heavenly appearance,
as well as heavenly designation, although committed to eternal
enmity towards God and His divine hosts. They were antithetical
in all ways excepting the retention of heavenly nomenclature, and
the archangels of Hell were always superior in rank and status to
common demons, as were those of Heaven.

Bearing in mind that Satan, or Lucifer, was *the* Christian lord
of Hell, Beelzebub was Prince of the First Hierarchy, but he was
also the *Crown* Prince of Hell, i.e., he was second in highest rank,
under Satan the Lord of Hell—which made him, in the terminology of the twentieth century when kings and princes have yielded
in most places to presidents and vice-presidents, vice-president
of Hell; or, as in some nations still retaining monarchies, prime
minister of Hell, under Satan, supreme Lord of Hell.

In his capacity as vice-president, or prime minister of Hell,
Beelzebub supervised the other hierarchies—but only in cases in-
volving a need for higher authority, otherwise each order and sub-
order was governed by its individual leader.

The second hierarchy was ruled by Carreau, the Prince of
Powers. Whereas Beelzebub's speciality was tempting men
with pride, most notably great men, kings, emperors, vain
rich men; Carreau's speciality was hardening human hearts, causing misery through mercilessness, overcoming feelings of compassion.

The third hierarchy was under Belias, Prince of Virtues. His
speciality was causing the downfall of mortals through arrogance.

He also encouraged women to mock God and church services, especially before children.

Every devil had an assigned 'choir' or order—or sub-order—but each devil did not necessarily specialize in the same variety of wickedness as the prince of his hierarchy, or even as the prince of his particular order. For example, although Belias (or Belial) was Prince of the Third Hierarchy, specializing in arrogance and contempt or ridicule, and had under him three lesser princes, who ruled the three orders of his hierarchy—virtues, archangels and angels—the minion-devils in these three orders were not required to limit themselves to either the speciality of Belias, or of the three lesser princes; they could, unless ordered otherwise, perform almost any evil act.

Balberith, as Prince of Cherubim (first hierarchy), fostered the idea of murder in men's minds; his minion-demons were noted for causing mortals to be quarrelsome, blasphemous, generally disagreeable, but the demons were not required to incite men to murder, although they often did.

Astaroth, Prince of Thrones (also first hierarchy) specialized in sloth, laziness, idleness. His demons caused discouragement among men; caused lassitude, indifference, irresponsibility.

Verrine, a lord of thrones under Astaroth, an example of a subaltern of Hell who ruled a sub-order of lesser—somewhat like novices—demons, specialized in temper, impatience, angry outbursts, sudden hot antagonisms.

Sonneillon, another lesser lord of a sub-order of thrones, under Astaroth, tempted men to sin through the wickedness of hatred against those who disagreed with them.

Each hierarchy had its prince, under Satan, and subject to the scrutiny of the crown prince, or prime minister, Beelzebub. Next below each prince were the three lords of the orders. Seraphim, cherubim, and thrones, in the first hierarchy, and each had a lesser prince, or lord. Under these lesser princes were the sub-orders, as many as were necessary for the maintenance of discipline and a sound organization.

Of the demons themselves, there were in the beginning no more in proportion to the number of mortals on earth than there were irreligious people, which meant there were few, no more possibly than a few thousand, perhaps not even that many. But in the beginning Christianity's faith was strong, its zealots many, as opposed to later times when the embers cooled and the number of heretics, apostates and outright materialistic pagans increased out of proportion to the number of devout, then Hell's orders had of necessity to inaugurate new sub-orders. It is this constant increment that creates most of the problems in defining the order and rank of devils, nor has it ever helped that *all* devils are inherently clever liars. Thus when Asmodeus, for example, was exorcized by a French priest during the Middle Ages, he was able to convince the exorcist that he had entered a nun's body to promote sloth and gluttony, when in fact, since his seduction of giddy Eve in the garden, Asmodeus had been notorious as a tempter towards amoral sexuality and he had entered the nun in order to tempt her with horrid—and fascinating—thoughts of sexual intercourse with an aged bishop.

Although under some circumstances, such as Solomon's ring, demons were compelled against their evil natures to be truthful— and from this fact came nearly all the information concerning them that chroniclers were able to record—by nature devils were notorious prevaricators.

In the Middle Ages, when exorcism flourished and great hosts of devils invaded earth, it was customary, upon ousting a devil, to demand of him his name, hierarchy, and order. It was usually considered dangerous, though, to engage exorcized devils in conversation or argument, although it was done often enough to verify, for example, that Oeillet was a devil of the order of dominions, second hierarchy, whose speciality was tempting holy men to break their vows of chastity and poverty; or that Rosier, a lesser dominion, also of the second hierarchy, tempted men to succumb to seduction, thus clearing the way for a succubus demon to steal their semen through unhallowed intercourse.

Of the three hierarchies of Hell, and their three orders, as well as the innumerable sub-orders or 'choirs', the princes and lesser princes, or lords, were rather firmly identified by the Middle Ages. Most *grimoires*, witch's handbooks, listed the princes, lords and particularities of each, as well as the names of many common devils who would, or who *had* at least, responded well and promptly when summoned by correct ritual, so that a witch or magician could rely upon Hell's aid when it was desired. But by

Anubis weighing the souls of the dead, from the Book of the Dead

Hades, the Greek Underworld, from an amphora showing Orpheus
subjugating Cerberus

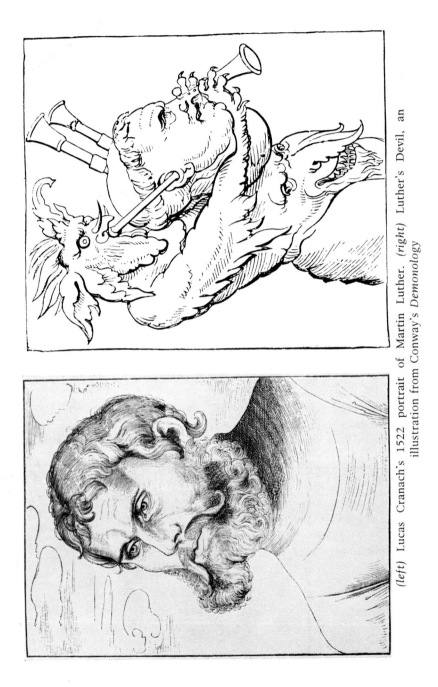

(left) Lucas Cranach's 1522 portrait of Martin Luther. *(right)* Luther's Devil, an illustration from Conway's *Demonology*

the Middle Ages there were hundreds of thousands of devils, so a complete roster, then or now, would be as enormous as a London or New York telephone directory. Such a directory would be unnecessary even for a witch or an exorcist. Spells, properly incanted and complemented, had only to be directed to the hierarchy, or to the order or sub-order, but, if these were unknown, then the appeal could be offered directly to the desired demon. In the event even this was unknown, then a spell directed to Satan, lord of Hell, outlining the contemplated wickedness—rape, murder, theft —would in theory result in a demon whose speciality concurred with the requirements, being ordered to manifest, and to aid in the commission of the *malefice*, or evil act.

The names were not usually as pronounceable as Beelzebub, Asmodeus, or Balberith, in any case. There was a devil named Sphendonael, another named Akephalos, a pair called Obizuth (who had only a head, no limbs or body) and Saphathorael.

In Collin de Plancy's 1863 version of the *Dictionnaire infernal*, Behemoth (first hierarchy, thrones) is shown in an illustration as possessing an elephant's head and legs, and an enormously distended stomach; he is of course a demon who tempts men to gluttony. Other illustrations show equally as repulsive demons, but it was never mandatory for a demon to appear in his normal shape although it *has* semed either obligatory or customary for them to give their proper names.

Anticif, Arfaxat, Calconix, Grongade, Enepsigos, Kunopegos, Leontophron were all devils who, at least once, were revealed on earth. The angels mentioned in the Kabbala who came to earth lusting after voluptuous Jewish maidens, and subsequently "were led astray and became corrupt in all their ways," were Sêmîazaz, Sariêl, Jomîaêl, Barâqijâl, Eẑeqêêl, Dânêl, Kôkabîêl, Arâkîbua, *et cetera*, and these were only eight of the ten leaders; there were many more.

Thus it has remained for many centuries an established fact that Hell's hierarchy consists of three hierarchies, each with three sub-divisions, or orders, below which are additional sub-orders, each governed by specific chieftains, all under the supreme rule of Satan, and alternately under Beelzebub as second lord of Hell, vice-president or prime minister, with each sub-order consisting— presently—of millions of zealot demons whose names are legion, but who can be categorized promptly and efficiently as to hierarchy and order, indicating that Christianity's Hell, far from being the place of utter chaos other underworlds have been in earlier millennia, is the product of ingenious organization, if it does not appear to be an epitome of discipline.

EIGHT

A Mixed Bag of Demons

The French jurist, Jean Bodin (1529–1596) who paradoxically denied the Divine Right of kings and favoured individual freedom and human dignity, on the one hand, and who, on the other hand, held that the law was justified in using any means from torture to deceit to gain confessions, wrote in 1580: "It is certain that the devils have a profound knowledge of all things. No theologian can interpret the Holy Scriptures better than they can; no lawyer has a more detailed knowledge of testaments, contracts and actions; no physician or philosopher can better understand the composition of the human body, and the virtues of the Heavens, the stars, birds and fishes, trees, herbs, metal and stones."

Johan Weyer, personal physician to the Duke of Cleves, a very learned man who lived between 1515 and 1588, and who was highly sceptical of church views of witchcraft and diabolism, nonetheless had this to say of the Devil: "Satan possesses great courage, incredible cunning, superhuman wisdom, the most acute penetration, consummate prudence, an incomparable skill in veiling the most pernicious artifices under a specious disguise, and malicious and infinite hatred toward the human race, implacable and incurable."

According to both these authorities—the first, Bodin, a willing convert to the belief that devils roamed the earth; the other, Weyer the Protestant, doubtful of such things—concurred in the conviction that Satan and his demons not only existed but constituted almost insurmountable obstacles to mankind.

They were not alone; a king of England (James I), a score of popes, at least nine-tenths of all clergymen, Catholic and Protestant, plus equally as many of the great minds of early and later Christianity, believed Satan and his demons were very real.

It was from this Christian intellectual galaxy that the theory and practice of Hell received its greatest impetus. Once the image of Satan was firmly established and officially recognized, 1,000 years of arduous spadework by Christianity's brightest luminaries created the best of all hierarchies of Hell. Solomon's *Testament*, the *Lemegeton* or lesser key of Solomon, all the *Clavicles*, the *Theurgia-Goetia*, Abano's *Heptameron*, all the old manuals, authentic or not (and how was one to prove they were, or were not?), that named demons and outlined profane rituals for summoning them, were excellent source-material for latter-day zealots.

Also, as the pagan gods were condemned to Hell, Christian popes and priests had at hand the ideal place for them, and to prove they were really devils the old names were kept.

In the *Lemegeton* spirits were named by the score. Their seals were given. "Demoriel", stated the *Lemegeton*, describing a particular spirit, "is the great and mighty Emprour of the North, who hath 400 great, and 600 Lesser Dukes with 700,000, 800,000, 900,000 servants under his command. . . ."

And again, with reference to another spirit of substance: ". . . when you Call Carnesiel, Either by day or Night there attends him 60.000.000.000 Dukes, but when you Call any of the dukes, there never attends above 300, and sometimes not above 10. . . ."

The numbers of Hell's inhabitants, using the old manuals and *grimoires* as sources, could be considered limitless. Christian theologians, leaning in part on old theories, and in part defining, or grouping, all devils according to Christianity's needs, chose a principal devil for each of the seven deadly sins: Satan for Anger, Belphegor for Sloth, Leviathan for Envy, Asmodeus for Lechery, Lucifer for Pride and Mammon for Avarice, etc., but these same theologians chose to classify devils less by actual hierarchy than by functions. Thus familiar demons were those that lived with and served mortals, while fates were demons dedicated to wrecking hopes, ambitions, aspirations. 'Clean' demons were titled thus because they appeared as very presentable entities. Their actual speciality was to frustrate, tempt and assail holy men.

Michael Psellus defined six varieties of devils and gave later Christian chroniclers their basis for saying that there were fiery demons who lived in the stratosphere, and who had no hand in evil on earth; aerial demons, who resided in the earthly ozone, and were destructive to man through winds, tempests, storms *et cetera*; terrestrial demons, who hid in forests, cities, boroughs, and occasionally disguised as men, went among mortals, doing great harm; aqueous demons, who resided in lakes, rivers, ponds, oceans, and because of their implacable hatred for mankind, brought death in the form of floods, great storms at sea, and so forth. When these aqueous devils took human form it was usually as women, because they enjoyed tempting men. The fifth category was the subterranean demons, who lived in caves, fissures, mountain crevasses. They specialized in injuring those mortals who worked in mines, who quarried stone, or who simply went hiking in the hills. They caused landslides, earthquakes, and forest fires. The sixth category had to do with heliophobic demons, those who could not abide light, and therefore came forth from the earth only at night. They killed wayfarers, maimed livestock, were violent by nature and despised all earth-life.

The actual hierarchy to which each devil belonged, although painstakingly plotted by early and late Christian chroniclers, lacked constancy. Belphegor could easily be confused with Balberith, while Belial and Belias—the latter, Prince of Virtues, third hierarchy—were liable to be categorized interchangeably.

But the labour of reconciling the lists was next to impossible. When Psellus wrote of his six groupings, for example, he literally left one, the fiery demons, up in the air. Guazzo's *Compendium Maleficarum*, published in 1608 and considered *nil plus ultra* for several centuries, said that Psellus's fiery demons "dwell in the upper air and will never descend to the lower regions until the Day of Judgment, and they have no dealings on earth with men". How, then, were these detached demons to be included among the hierarchies of Hades, which was deep in the earth? For that matter, how could Guazzo or Psellus even be certain fiery demons *were* demons?

Then, too, there was a good bit of weeding-out to be done. Even Solomon's *Testament* did not confine itself to enumerating only evil spirits. In fact the "sons of God [who] saw the daughters of men that they were fair; and they took them wives of all which they chose" (Genesis vi, 2) and who were further eulogized in the Kabbala for their fall and ultimate alleged iniquities, were closer to being creditable teachers than lechers. True, according to legend they lusted after "the daughters of men", and even formed an unangelic conspiracy to achieve seduction. "And they were in all two hundred, who descended in the day of Jared . . . took unto themselves wives, and they began to go in unto them and to defile themselves with them"; but aside from the fact that these "daughters of men" became pregnant and in due course "bare giants whose height was three thousand ells", the angels taught mankind "charms and enchantments, and the cutting of roots, and made them acquainted with plants".

The fact that the giant offspring of these unions later vexed the race of man did not, in reverse of phophecy, work the evils of the sons upon the fathers. The fathers brought a great deal of good to earth, thus they could not be categorically condemned to Hell; at least it should have been unlikely they could qualify, having done good among men, as benign devils, although, since Hell was a limitless place, their names were ultimately found in some hellish lists, perhaps placed there by celibate priests to whom the venial sin of seduction was by itself unpardonable.

The process of elimination, however, was handily resolved by Christianity through the accepted process of relegating to Hell anyone whose name was associated with other theologies, and as a result of this consistent policy, in time Hell became inhabited by a mixed bag of demons, not only too numerous to name, but also too complex to be correctly catalogued.

So large was Hell's population that by the Middle Ages when the *Rituale Romanun*, the exorcist's routine, was formally in effect throughout Western Europe, and despite a number of written definitions of Hell's hierarchy, the only certain way for priests to know with which devil they were struggling was to demand his name, rank, and hierarchy. All the learned authorities did not agree in their written compendiums, and in many cases when the exorcized demon gave his name, he was found not to be known to any of the lists, or to be known by several names. Apollyon, for example was also listed by a Hebrew name for a destroyer, Abaddon (Revelations, ix, 11), and Belial were listed also as Lucifer, while such names as Decarabia, Goap, Ipos, Cimejes, Andrealphus, Raum and Orobas appeared, some known, some unheard of prior to an exorcism, at least to many Christian clerics.

Belial, the Jewish apocalyptic name for a chief lord of evil, defined as "the 68th spirit" of Hell, was often confused with Baal, Berith, Beale and Bolfry, by Christian chroniclers. Only such established demons as Asmodeus, with a long record of interesting sensuality, or Astoroth, who also derived from ancient mythology and came ready-made into the pantheon of Christianity's Hell, were sufficiently historic to survive unaltered. Of these demons of long-standing many came to Hell by way of ancient Phoenicia: Dagon, Baaltis, Ashtoreth (Astoroth), Melkarth and Moloch, Baal, Onca, Hadad and Eshmun, among others. But even this was no guarantee they could survive individually, when, for instance, those who could so easily interpret the Latin word *lamia* meaning witch, into an anglicized word meaning 'screech-owl'; and who did not speak, read, or evidently comprehend the language of ancient Phoenicia; and who wrote in Latin for Germans, English-men, Scandinavians and others who did not know Latin; tried to create intelligible lists for all Christians. They could not possibly do so, but even if they had been able, the learned ecclesiastics of those other lands, speaking other languages, could not interpret properly.

Then there was also wholesome bias. England's Protestants, while perfectly willing to accept Satan and all his demons, chose also not to accept Catholic France or Spain or Italy as supreme authority and conjured up not quite a separate hierarchy but a respectably numerous 'choir' of ethnically English demons, among whom were such entities as the 'luggard fiend', and any number of 'bar-gheists' who, while evil, could occasionally be out-witted, and came in time more to resemble sprites than devils.

Adding to the inconsistency, not to mention the confusion, was the known fact that devils rarely appeared in normal form. Every devil seemed to have an affinity for a particular disguise, or per-haps it was the situation that required a particular manifestation. As some said, and quite reasonably, a humble crofter could hardly escape detection as an ally of Satan if some bizarre creature, with a tail, wings, and possibly even horns upon his head, came to live at the cottage. On the other hand it was entirely acceptable if the crofter acquired, for example, a large black dog, a crow, a calico cat, even a toad or spider, and these disguises were common among devils.

Devils frequently assumed human form. They also fashioned

simulated human likenesses from the air. Michael Psellus, whose work in the cataloguing of devils achieved circulation and acceptance in both Protestant and Catholic lands, said that demons could form bodies for themselves ". . . from semen and its odour when men and women copulated"; hence there appeared to be no limit and no restrictions on the materials available to devils from which to create disguises, and inevitably people who feared devils saw them everywhere, in all manner of forms and substances. Francis Barrett, author of an 1801 book entitled *The Magus or Celestial Intelligencer*, although arriving several centuries too late to make an impression among the great demonologists, not only changed the order and function of devils, he also restricted them somewhat—but too late, for their numbers had become so great that no single demonologist, certainly not one belonging to the eighteenth or nineteenth centuries, could affect any appreciable or acceptable change.

By the nineteenth century the hierarchy had been fairly well standardized, at least from the 'Emprour' down through the chairs to the subordinate orders and sub-orders; but the enumeration, the individual directory of devils, because it was constantly, even daily and hourly, being added to, was subject to whatever additions anyone like Francis Barrett cared to suggest.

But for Barrett to alter that which had been established for centuries, and so late, guaranteed only Barrett's own neglect. Mammon, for example, the devil who made men evil through wealth, and who was for centuries renowned for this speciality, under Barrett became a devil who tempted and trapped men through deceit. Asmodeus, whose speciality even prior to his adoption by Christians, had always been amoral sexuality, under Barrett became an avenger in the service of common witches and sorcerers.

The devils survived Barrett; so did Hell's hierarchy. Even Barrett's additions to the roster of devils was neglected. Pythos, Barrett's lord of lies, did not acquire a foothold; Hell had a prince of lies of long-standing, although a specialist was hardly required since commonly and by virtue of vocation all devils were accomplished liars.

Of the hierarchy, little could be added to it, or expounded about it, that had not already been said or written from the first century A.D. through the seventeenth century. But of the brigades, corps, legions of devils, which was, like Bolivar's army, a great sack with a hole in the bottom, there was always room for comment. St. Macarius of Alexandria prayed to God to permit him to see Satan's hosts. God acquiesced and St. Macarius beheld a hair-raising spectacle of devils "as numerous as bees". In the year 1459 the demonologist Alphonsus de Spina was convinced that fully one-third of all the angels of Heaven had fallen, had become devils. His total for that choir of angels was 133,306,668. Others gave lesser or greater numbers. Several authorities claimed that the princes alone numbered 66, 72, and 79, which is relevant only in relation to the number of orders and sub-orders under each prince. By the closing decades of the fifteenth century it was thought that not less than half of the world's population, including the living who were damned and the dead who had already gone below, belonged to Satan.

Since those times five centuries have passed. There has also been a great increase in mankind's general disillusionment with religion; if not outright denunciation of faith, then at the least a widespread neglect of it. On such a basis it might not be unreasonable to assume that by the declining decades of the twentieth century, two-thirds or nine-tenths of mankind will belong to Satan—an unsettling hypothesis because it implies that in the end evil will triumph over good. But this in itself need not be entirely regrettable, for by then the intellectual gymnastics of many philosophers who have held that good is a relative condition, will be proven. That which is thought to be good now—caring for the aged, the orphaned, the lame and blind, seeking brotherhood among men, acknowledging a God—will become evil. The good will become that which is relative to the desires of Satan's plurality: killing the disabled, enslaving minorities, acknowledging Satan the Lord.

The balance of power between good and evil since earliest times has been acknowledgeably in the balance. Satan, with his mixed bag of demons has never relented, has never rested on a seventh day. He has not yielded and he has not slept. He is older than Christianity, and more subtle than its learned wisemen. For millennia beyond recall he has zealously raked in those of all theologies who have been the fallen. In all that time he has released no more than a handful. Pagan gods and the Christian Saviour visited Hell and came away shaken and emptied. During those visits, before and afterwards, the endless hordes arrived by the thousands, by the tens of thousands, brought low by the events neither Osiris in his prime, Ahura-Mazda at his zenith, or Jesus Christ at his best, could prevent: famine, flood, drought, pestilence, war, and over-population.

NINE

Some Altered Aspects of Devils

Stratification has never had relevance except to dying things. Its antithesis, change, in its most common form has historically been accommodation.

For example, the early Christians celebrated Christ's birth on 6th January. The 25th December was a pagan date set aside for celebrating the sun's nativity. There were many more pagans than Christians. It was simply good business to change Christ's birth date and through this accommodation bring about a gradual conversion of the pagans to Christianity. For those who persisted in celebrating on 6th January, the festival of Epiphany was inaugurated; thus no one was really the loser, although through change Christianity was surely the winner.

Inevitably, then, Satan and his demons were also required to change. If the minions of Hell were to survive, they also had to modernize.

All the old lords of Hell, as well as the old gods that belonged to specific ethnic or national cosmogonies, and whose characteristics were exclusive to those cosmogonies, perished when, and not infrequently before, the cultures to which they belonged also perished. If any of them were resurrected by ensuing theologies, almost without exception it was to a new existence not as gods but as devils. But the great majority never rose at all.

If it was possible to degrade powerful Zeus, chief god of the Greeks, the most widely known name for an ultimate, supreme deity among the ancient Indo-Europeans; then it was possible to bring anyone down. It did not have to be some hoary pagan god, it could be a mortal man, a lord, a scholar, even a king, but, whoever or whatever he had been, once he was consigned to Hell he became an evil demon changer from whatever he had been before and destined to remain changed as long as Hell lasted.

But this change from God, or man, to devil, did not mean that the fallen individual was fixed in form or substance, it meant that he was fixed in *purpose*. Henceforth his total motivation was to augment, generate, encourage and tirelessly serve, evil. He was dedicated to the destruction of God and of man.

As a demon he was "completely inscrutable and of a character beyond human comprehension". He was incapable of good deeds or compassionate thoughts. He was "dark within, shaken with icy passions, malicious, restless and perturbed". As such an entity he could very easily move ahead with man, his enemy, but in order to do so he had to accommodate himself to all man's changes.

In Rome after Romulus demons moved rather gradually from the countryside to the cities, their labours having less to do with bringing on storms to flatten crops, or ailments to wither kine, than they had to do with ruining the business or political aspirations of merchants, nobles and soldiers.

In earlier times the Phoenician god Dagon, who was later associated with Israel, seems to have at one time enjoyed great popularity throughout Western Asia. He was a fish-god long before he became a Christian devil. The early Assyrians said Dagon had a "form resembling that of a fish, but with a human head growing below the fish's [head] and with human feet growing alongside the fish's tail and growing out of it."

It is entirely plausible that Dagon's name derived from the Phoenician *dag*, meaning fish, although by the time Dagon had matriculated, had become part of the Scriptural scene where he, as a Philistine called Dagon, fell on his face before the ark, he was no longer associated with fish. Still later, exorcized from a nun in the Middle Ages, Dagon's change was complete; he was a demon of Hell.

Asmodeus, that sly old devil who seduced Eve and ravished fair Sara, was not always such a lecher. The *Lemegeton* noted that "Asmoday" was a "great King, Strong and Powerful . . . with three heads, where of the first is like a Bull, the second like a Man, the third like a Ram . . . his foot is webbed like a Goose, he sitteth on an Infernall Dragon . . . he giveth the Ring of Vertues, he teacheth the art of Arithmetick Geometry Astronomy and all handcrafts absolutely, he giveth true answers to your Demands...."

Change came and in order to survive Asmodeus became evil in the Book of Tobit, deflowering Sara, and after that his altered aspect was rapid. He became a proud and disdainful demon dedicated to preventing marriages and inciting to adultery. So renowned was he that the Christians borrowed him in total, lechery and all, and he became in their category of Hell a seraphim of the first hierarchy, whose duty was "to tempt men with his swine of luxuriousness". He was said to be a "prince of wantons", and by the year 1643 was exorcized by a French priest of Louviers from a nun, Sister Elizabeth.

For Asmodeus the change from scholar to evil demon was complete; he was frequently revealed as one of Satan's most energetic disciples and, like Dagon, was tireless in the furtherance of his speciality, adultery, amorality of all kinds, and presently divorce.

Generally, all demons, like those of early Rome, had to abandon their former ways of life and adjust to the alterations in the lives of their hosts and enemies. The fiends of Olde England who had at one time been content to reside in dark forests or caves, or black pools and ruined stone residences, waiting for luckless wayfarers, were required to move into towns and villages, eventually into great cities. Also, although when they appeared among the Romans disguised as mortals, they were required to assume the sandals and robes of Rome; in a latter-day France and Germany, in human form they appeared in trousers, blouses, caps, adapting whatever attire was regionally endemic. Further, they of necessity not only had to use the prevalent language—which was never an obstacle, devils by tradition being glib and gifted linguists—but they had to accommodate themselves to the reasoning, the thinking processes of later times, as well.

The Devil who sat in Collin de Plancy's bedchamber naked except for the trident he held, was a physically powerful individual, man-like except for horns and tail, very erudite and co-operative, never at a loss for the correct thing to say, full of artful justifications, and rather admirable in his logic. He was not at all like vicious and repugnant old Charun whom the Etruscans so dreaded.

Another deity of antiquity who had no difficulty in making the transition, and whose adaptability may have been facilitated by his age, was the demon Asiel, or Aziel, whose name lent itself to probably as many variations in spelling as that of any other demon.

Originally, Asiel was named in an historic Greek papyri as a magical angel, but he evidently came into the Greek pantheon from the Chaldean theology which designated him as a spirit of metallurgy—although, as Eliza Butler suggests in her *Ritual Magic* (1949), it is possible that he descended from the Akkadian cosmos.

He was mentioned in the Kabbala, with the implication that he, as one of the fallen angels of Genesis, came to earth among the 200 who "lusted after" the daughters of men. As Asael—and Azazel—he "taught men to make swords, and knives, and shields, and breastplates, and made known to them the metals and the art of working them". He had not changed his affinity, only his status; he was still knowledgeable in the field of metallurgy. It was this gift that made Asiel recognizable, but later, when he became the demon familiar of Doctor Faust, it was said that he was also, along with being Hell's foremost metallurgist, one of Satan's Grand Dukes—which would seem to place him too high in the hierarchy to serve Faust or anyone else as a mere familiar. Still, an invocation for summoning him appears often in the different *grimoires*, or black books of the magicians, always with the implication that Asiel can bring gold to the mortal willing to barter his soul in exchange for it. Thus Asiel, no matter how he had changed, in other ways, remained associated with metal.

Johann Faust exalted Asiel, having him contend, and successfully, with the demon Mephistophiel; and another time when he was summoned, his fury was aroused and he killed two Germans and nearly killed a third whose greed overcame their good sense at the invocation. As a murderer Asiel appeared savage and unregenerate, a thorough evil demon of Hell. But throughout, he remained the devil to be invoked for riches accruing from metal. In later times this meant gold almost exclusively. He shared with other devils a power of divination for the recovery of buried treasure, which implied that his change from the days of the Fall, when he taught men to forge weapons and make breastplates, was easy; he came to be associated with precious metals rather than with the base ones. By the Middle Ages even a Marshal of France, Gilles de Rais, was capable of appreciating Asiel's capabilities in the field of repairing squandered fortunes by revealing where gold lay, either in its natural state or as hidden treasure.

Devils such as Asiel, Asmodeus and Dagon seemed to master Christianity's theology without any difficulty. They could expound abstract cosmogony with the most learned clerics, argue rationally with popes and kings, or confound humble but learned monks, almost out of hand.

The number of disputes between theologians and devils seemed almost limitless, particularly during the epoch of the Reformation. It was indeed a sad churchman who could not announce having had at least one resounding argument with a devil. Fame came to many such mortal men, not all churchmen, for ultimately the nobles, even the peasants, although it was unwise, often downright dangerous for low people to usurp this prerogative of their betters, had conversations with wights.

Exorcized demons were especially susceptible to interrogation and dispute with mortals. Also, as the records suggest, exorcized demons were only rarely genuinely reluctant. In the year 1618, a team of exorcists, Jesuits, Capuchins, and Dominicans, relieved a noble woman of a devil named Magot, in the chapel of Notre-Dame-de-Guerison, and four days later they expelled another demon, who obligingly identified himself as "Mahonin, of the third hierarchy [sic] . . . and that his living, before he entered the body of the possessed, was in the water".

At other exorcisms, demons argued against expulsion, quoting Scripture, Christian history, and even their divine right, as being incapable of producing evil without God's sanction. More than one cleric was bested in arguments with devils, these revelations being attested to by members of the Catholic faith when recounting such meetings between Protestants and demons, as well as by monks of one order verifying instances of devils debating with monks of other orders.

Any number of rural ministers in both Europe and the United States had encounters with glib demons, and at least once in relatively recent times an exorcized devil caused a fatal ailment to blight an exorcist.

The altered aspects went further. As the church grew strong and wealthy, practically unassailable in its power, and as national states, for several reasons, adopted state religions, devils either in human form or through the feat of demoniacal possession began to be discovered among those who, in Catholic lands, questioned Church policy and edict, or those who, in Protestant lands, questioned king or clergy. When exorcism failed, as it did, actually, more often than it succeeded, the alternatives were imprisonment or the stake, and when reasonable people questioned the torture-death of some dissenter possessed of an evil demon, the common reply was that if a human being had to perish in order to thwart a devil, it was not an exorbitant price to pay.

These possessing devils kept abreast of their times. They also demonstrated sagacity by only rarely appearing as they normally, or naturally, were endowed to appear, and every disguise was tailored to the times. For example, as the years passed and the vastly respected but much earlier dragon diminished as a creditable creature, devils opted for more modern manifestative forms.

Imps, the lowest order of devils, endowed with a specific inherent crudeness, and actually incapable of finesse, were less likely to use disguises. Commonly, imps appeared more or less as they were, and because this meant they appeared naked, their manifestation ordinarily created some degree of consternation, particularly in such surroundings as those provided for in convents and schools.

But imps had probably less difficulty in adjusting to change than did other devils, of higher orders, because an imp was solely concerned with basic evil. It did not matter what period in history was current, imp-antics were applicable; they were constant, often painful, always embarrassing, never more lofty or devious than causing a mortal to trip and fall, to spill food on someone at a banquet, perhaps to forget to zip up. Imps were practically impervious to the physical changes among mortals; their purpose, like their presence, involved only annoying triviality, and for that neither imagination nor erudition were necessary.

In historic times when people lived together for protection, and were more or less restricted in movement, their deities as well as their devils were localized. Trees and stones were inhabited by these powerful and invisible entities, as were lakes, ponds, fens and valleys. Aaron's wand, for example, when stuck into the ground to prove its magic, took root and bore fruit. Historic writings abound with reference to this sceptre—it was through its magic, in fact, that Lilith was able to obtain her wings and escape from Adam in the Garden, and it was because Moses, a fugitive wanted for murder at the time, was able to uproot the tree that he won his wife, Zipporah—but legends aside, stones and trees, lakes and mountains, contained devils and deities. But when the communes of early man began to disintegrate, as weapons, boats, the means of travel and defence improved, making it possible for sedentary commune—dwellers to forage farther afield and making it possible for them to find better homes in distant places, the difficulty arising from transporting great stones or of transplanting aged trees created a crisis.

It was not possible to bring the olden rock-bound and tree-dwelling gods, good and evil, to the new place. They had to be liberated from their stones and trees, and many were; but only the devils were capable of making this adjustment *en masse*. Many of the gods remained behind—a god whose purpose was to bring warmth and sunshine in a cold climate was no longer needed by people migrating to a temperate or hot area.

But the evil among people remained practically unchanged. Treachery, avarice, hatred, dishonesty, all the devil-inspired torments, existed in the new place exactly as each had existed in the old place. The devils, perhaps altered in aspect, and certainly altered in new-found liberation and mobility, accomplished the transition with little difficulty. Each time the tribe moved, its demons moved with it; each time there was a change in fortune, in theology, in all the aspects of slow progress from the cave to the hovel, to the village and castle, to the town and manor-house, the devils kept pace. The gods more often than not were neglected or substantially changed, but not the devils; their basic image, although in fresh or difficult attire, was unaltered. All that was required of them was that in their constancy of purpose, they served evil.

Except for this, Asmodeus, for example, could not have survived any longer than did Jupiter; Asiel could not have survived the long-since-forgotten black sun or the Akkadian cosmos, and Satan would not have remained strong and flourishing after the demise of disagreeable old Charun, and the Etruscan Novensiles.

The sacred groves were forgotten, the sprites and dryads and loftier deities perished through neglect. The Druids of the Celts

F

died out, as did the tree-deities of Upsake in Sweden. All that survived were devils. Every other ancient entity atrophied through neglect, survived as a devil in Hell, or simply ceased to have relevance and power, as happened with Nicolaus, 'destroyer of the people', who became a ludicrous caricature called something else—in this instance, jolly old Santa Claus.

Demons, of all the entities that ever influenced mankind, were able to keep abreast of all change. They and Satan are older than all the theologies; they have in fact grown stronger, not weaker, increasing in power and influence as the ages of man have over-lapped one another. And as the numbers of mankind has increased, the population of Hell has grown until it can rival the numbers of Heaven without difficulty—there have always been more sinners than saints, and now there are also more devils to harrow earth, than there have ever been angelic hosts to save it.

TEN

The Subject of Influence

The early Church's preoccupation with Hell and Satan equalled its interest in salvation. There was of course an obvious corollary, but there were times, particularly between the years 1450 and 1750, when salvation appeared to run a poor second.

Nor was the subject of influence confined to the church. A number of notables ranging in power and importance from kings to burghers succumbed either to ecclesiastical blackmail or to the secret importunings of Satan's advocates among the living. At least one Marshal of France, Gilles de Laval, Baron de Rais, charged with a grisly array of sexual perversions against children, was actually strangled, then burned, for greater crimes. It was alleged that he "adored and sacrificed to spirits, conjured them and made others conjure them, and wished to make a pact with the said evil spirits, and by their means to have and to receive, if he could, knowledge, power and riches".

Among lesser people, any hint of paganism was in the church's view, proof that Satan was at work, although Christianity was a very long time in reaching many of the isolated areas of Western Europe, and even after it had reached them, many an old Norse or Teutonic god, or devil, was either exorcized or propitiated by the wild fires lit on hilltops on Walpurgis Night, the eve of May Day.

Satan's influence extended to the prudent in medieval times exactly as it had occurred to prehistoric man. If God was good and salvation depended largely upon repentance, and if the Devil was vindictively unregenerate and adamant, then it was only simple prudence to placate the Devil, and to seek forgiveness, provided one did not die very suddenly, at one's leisure, thus managing to achieve a measure of security during the mortal sojourn and also being assured of salvation after death.

It was a hard life any way one looked at it. For early man all the world beyond the cave's entrance was hostile, the night most of all, for after daylight faded demons of incredible ferocity and slyness came, very often without sound or form or substance, to suck the blood or steal one's soul, and obviously God was indifferent, otherwise He would have protected man.

Later, in biblical times, when man was capable of writing his thoughts, of disseminating them, all that had really changed was that the indifferent God then became "a terrible and mighty", a God who would have no other Gods before Him, and in a sense He was very like His enemy the Lord of Hell. His fury was implacable, His compassion uncertain, His vengeance fierce and swift.

The Church made it abundantly clear that damnation, like Damocles' sword, hung overhead, held by the merest thread. Mortal man, it was averred, was born a sinner and could not escape a sinner's fate. He arrived in this world bearing guilt for what his presumed predecessors had done in the Garden of Eden, and in those times, although it was said that by the Middle Ages he had come far, the fact is that he had hardly advanced at all, either spiritually or materially. At the time of the First Crusade great lords often slept on straw scattered over stone floors. Men ate with their fingers, frequently several using the same bowl. European bread in those times was coarse, usually stale and mealy. Fields were ploughed by hand, the yield was meagre, half went to the armed nobles, and every year starvation claimed thousands; and even in those times of unbelievable filth and squalor, the population was usually well ahead of the development of arable land.

European productivity was largely the result of handicraft. What people needed, except for the very wealthy who were an exception, they made for themselves or secured through barter, theft, or warfare.

Travel was disorganized, extremely hazardous, and avoided except by armed bodies, either of soldiers or caravaneers, and it was also ruinously expensive. Wealth was measured less in money than in the thickness of one's residential walls. There were no sewer systems, bathing was thought to be unhealthy, leprosy was common and syphilis was both prevalent and socially acceptable. The average life-span was thirty-five years.

Candles, although popularly accredited in illustrations of those times as being a major source of light, were rare. Resin torches were much more prevalent because candles were too expensive, especially for some of the larger castles. Resin torches gave off smoke and light in equal parts.

Man was the measure of all things in those times. His strength, his intelligence, and his crippling ignorance, were the yardstick by which all things were measured. His world was almost entirely an agrarian one. He knew little of medicine, less of natural law, and nothing at all of things which subsequent ages took for granted such as germs, sanitation, proper treatment of stored foodstuffs, and, although he was periodically decimated by them, plagues and pestilence. Even the agriculture of the Middle Ages in Europe was inferior to the agriculture of Gallo-Roman times.

Most important of all, in medieval times the Church was powerful. It did not, actually, wage a great spiritual war for the redemption or the salvation of souls in Europe, although its historians have said that it did; and because it did not, pockets of paganism flourished for centuries.

The Church was far more concerned with strengthening or augmenting its power than with saving the souls of a peasantry which was both abysmally superstitious and despised. Bishops and abbots sought wealth and power first; and during those ages when it was impossible to keep these things against those rapacious brigands, the armed and lusty secular nobility, the ecclesiastical lords' second obligation was to buy and support armed Church garrisons.

From this lasting competition between bishops and lords, kings and popes, evolved a condition that prevailed even before medieval times, when salvation came second after politics, with the result that even the enlightened nobility were sceptical of a god thus served and represented; while the lower classes, merchants, seamen, crofters, those forming the ignorant majority, tradesmen and peasants—fearful of Catholic power, which was very great—were a very long time abandoning their friendly nymphs and fairies and kindly undines.

Nor did it help the cause of conversion that the language of the Church was Latin. Even in Latin countries this was a language no longer understood. It *did* foster and encourage unity *within* the Church, where Italians, Frenchmen, Germans, Spaniards *et al.* had a common basis for understanding. But the Bible, the Gospels, patristic comment, all written or, like Mass, spoken in Latin, additionally contributed not to alienation (because many had never been converted), but to the kind of supra-national, internal Church unity that made laymen of all nations and classes aware that God's Church was a world apart.

In times of travail it was common for men to return to the small, simple and personal gods, not all of whom were entirely virtuous; and when an outraged clergy denounced this practice as heresy, and the old gods as demons, by and large all that resulted was that paganism, instead of retreating, went underground, and the influence of the demons continued.

In time it was even possible for a strong current of diabolism to be discernible despite the Church's energetic use of the sword, torch, and torture chamber to bring forcible conversion. In a world where armed men rode triumphant, and where the vaunted humility of Christianity resulted in varieties of physical torture worse than that suffered by Christ at Calvary, Satan, not Jesus, held forth hope, and Satan's influence was strong—stronger by far, on earth where the agony prevailed, than the humility and divine passion of a Saviour whose representatives did not even speak in an understandable language.

Heretic groups emerged in such divergent locales as Spain and Scandinavia. The Church retaliated with prompt and organized vigour. It had laws against sorcery based upon the Biblical edict "Thou shalt not suffer a witch to live", but in fact the earlier laws were neither stringent nor enforced. However, the Devil's influence had reached a stage, by the year 1200, of considerable magnitude, and the Vatican sent forth inquisitors who reported that heresy was everywhere and increasing. These inquisitors did *not* note that the reason for this was a rather general anti-Church sentiment based on clerical immorality and authoritarianism, nor that as the Church hunted down and persecuted its enemies, it also to a great degree created the very enemies it sought. Nor did the high prelates suggest that the writings of a number of the Church's own exalted personages—particularly the works of St. Catherine of Siena, St. Bonaventure and St. Bernard—might be examined to find the reason for this growing apostasy.

The Devil was clearly testing his strength by encouraging people to ask questions whose answers had to be heretical. Also, repressive, rich and powerful abbots whose doctrinal authority was absolute, backed by pikes and axes, appeared in the eyes of peasants no different, even in their way of life and in their bloody punishment of troublemakers. Hundreds of thousands of people were put to death for the "salvation of their souls".

Repression in any age, with or without the involvement diabolic influence, only insured additional insurgency, and the trickle of heresy became a flood. The Church's answer was a number of papal bulls which authorized an official Inquisition whose purpose was to seek, examine, and exterminate European heretics. In the thirteenth century a sect, the Manichaens of Albi, in southern France (subsequently referred to as Albigensians), who believed in a God who was both good and evil and who condoned sexual promiscuity, came to Church attention. Another sect, in the same locale, known as Waldensians (or Vaudois), who chose to believe the Bible, not the Pope, was God's ultimate authority on earth, was also attacked.

The Devil lost both contests, if, as the Church averred, he was behind the Manichaens and the Waldensians. Church power and pikes nearly wiped out both sects. It also managed to secure for Church coffers considerable heretic wealth in the process.

In the fourteenth century an aroused and well-armed Inquisition broke the Knights Templars whose secret society the Church had reason to fear. The knights were not only landed, wealthy, and growing in power, they also questioned Church motives. Among other things, the knights were accused of performing the *osculum infame*, or kissing Satan's arse as part of their unforgivable heresies.

The Devil was in disarray before the swords and torches of Christ's Church, his influence, however, seemed only to abate in respect of strong organized bodies. Thereafter, according to zealot inquisitors, he sent legions of demons abroad to recruit individual heretics, and during the ensuing three centuries his alleged converts were burned, tortured to death, and exterminated to the number of about half a million human beings, among whom were thousands of women who had had sexual intercourse with Satan, clergymen who were appalled at the enormity of this holy murder, lords, ladies, tradesmen of wealth whose riches were appropriated by clerics as part of their punishment, and a great many luckless Protestants who fell into Catholic hands during the Inquisition's long tenure. The Devil, obviously, was everywhere, while his demons by the thousands came forth from Hell to join in the struggle against, not just God, Jesus, and the Pope, but also against mankind in general.

The surest way for Catholicism to prove diabolism was to allege that a heretic knew Satan or his devils, and the best way to accomplish this was to charge the accused in clerical courts where no rebuttal was allowed. Satan, although subpoenaed, never appeared, and in fact the Church had to invent advocates. But one fact appeared clear: after many centuries as a Lord of Darkness, as an ugly, malevolent entity who appeared only in death-chambers to gather a soul, or as a lofty daemon who contended only on hallowed levels against other gods; Satan as a formidable organizer, strategist, and Commander-in-Chief of armies of devils, had come into his own, prepared finally to join battle against God and man for supremacy on earth and in Heaven, his influence great and his power formidable.

The Inquisition shed light on Satan's wickedness in many ways. It was proved that lonely old women who kept a cat, or perhaps a bird or chicken, were in fact actually harbouring demons disguised as animals; and it was also proved that dissident nuns and prioresses were secretly Satan's concubines, defiling themselves through sexual abominations with imps and demons.

So great did Satan's influence become that in Protestant lands inquisitorial judges copied all the Catholic precedents, even the one that permitted no defence of an accused satanist on the grounds that those who defended themselves or others against a charge of heresy were themselves engaging in it.

In 1257 Pope Innocent IV approved the use of torture against heretics, and later popes supported and strengthened this edict. It was not abolished by the Vatican until 1816, and while it was in force men screamed out their secrets about pacts with Satan, and women died by the thousands from tortures that forced from them similar confessions.

The result of all this was that even good Christians were alienated, and those who had resisted conversion, as well as many, among them a large number of Protestants, who had tolerated

Church edicts and policies in the past, turned away from Catholicism in droves. Thus the Church was in the position of fighting a fire it had started. What kept this increasing host of enemies from destroying the Church was that while they were never organized, the Church's supporters, Catholic kings, emperors, great lords, *were* organized, and medieval Europe was a warrior-lord's paradise.

Satan, it would be claimed in aftertimes, really was not beaten. Satan had infiltrated the Church itself; had influenced Church policies until they served his purpose, which had always been the destruction of man; had influenced the popes to use their power to alienate Christians from their Saviour; had succeeded through his consummate wiles in bringing Christianity's God into disrepute even among Christians. He had successfully caused Church policy in conjunction with secular authority, to destroy mortal heroes—Joan of Arc, accused of hearing 'voices' which it was alleged were of demoniacal origin, among others—and Satan's hordes, circulating throughout Christianity, by employing diabolic logic, furthered the designs of their Lord by causing a few courageous men to denounce the Holy Inquisition, whose sole purpose was to stamp out evil and heresy to the Glory of God.

ELEVEN

The Devil's Advocates

Those who most notably served Satan in mythology and natural history, from earliest to recent times, were commonly those who had earned the recognition, often the respect and admiration, of their contemporaries. But this usually only obtained in one place. Jesus was the Son of God to Christians; they worshipped him in Jerusalem, and later as His cult spread, so did the homage. But to non-Christians—and not just the pagans of Christianity's early years—Jesus was considered a necromancer, a sorcerer, an evil person, a mortal who could speak with the dead, a preacher who called down God's wrath on unbelievers. In short, this Man was considered in many parts of the world either an embodiment of evil, or possibly even Satan himself.

To Mohammedans He was rarely thought of as a myth, the way Christians thought of the Gods of Greece and Rome. When His blood-red cross appeared in the van of the zealot Crusader hordes, it was not difficult to imagine Him as the evil inspiration of evil men. Even when the Church of Rome sent forth its Inquisitors, much later, no one scoffed at the improbability of His earlier, mortal existance, but many noted that what was done in His name was satanic in its cruelty.

He was, for a great many of the world's non-Christians—who were always vastly more numerous than Christians—the Devil's advocate; what He inspired in His most devout followers caused anguish even in Christian lands. Even among Christians there was a feeling that when calamity occurred, it only did so with Divine acquiescence, and that went back to the very ancient, non- or pre-Christian idea that God had a dual nature, equally good and equally bad.

For Satan, to whom every evil was attributed, and who was

never thought of as even temporarily or marginally 'good', this rationale added a continuum of substantiation. *He existed.*

During the exacerbated controversy known as the Reformation, Protestants related how Dr. Johann Faust, after making his pact with Satan, visited the Vatican with his invisible associate Mephistopheles, and the Pope could never exorcize the devil nor gain mastery over Faust. The Catholics, on the other hand, implied that Faust, as Satan's advocate, had influenced Martin Luther in the very city where Luther nailed his theses to the church door.

Luther, himself, saw Satan everywhere, and while the Reformation gave impetus to the idea that devils did not have to be individual entities, but could in fact be found in personal and private wicked thoughts and individual harmful actions, Martin Luther never yielded his conviction that Satan was far from being an abstraction.

The Reformation, schism that it was, with many remaining faithful to Rome's spiritual supremacy, and many others (Protestants) in loud protest, clamouring for reforms, split Europe and sorely troubled all Christians. The Reformation strengthened Satan, as must be the case with any house divided, with each division charging that the other obtains strength from a common enemy.

No period in Christian history was even so beneficial to the Devil. He had advocates on both sides, including Martin Luther, who wrote in his *Tishreden* that, "Early this morning when I awoke the fiend came and began disputing with me. 'Thou art a great sinner,' said he. I replied, 'Canst not tell me something new, Satan?' "

Luther viewed the Pope as the Devil's advocate and the Roman Church as the Devil's kingdom. He never for a moment doubted Satan's individual existence. Once, while working at his Bible, Luther allegedly saw Satan grinning scornfully at him from the shadows and hurled an inkstand at him. In Luther's denunciations Satan as a real, "living power, a concrete personality", as Dr. Paul Carus said in his *History of the Devil* (1900), gained not only stature, but confirmation of his existence was reaffirmed by the leading Protestant of the Reformation. He was God's instrument of punishment, and although evil undoubtedly lurked in the hearts of men, it only did so because Satan, the demon not the abstraction, had planted it there. Luther wrote:

> And were this world with devils filled,
> That threaten to undo us;
> We will not fear, for God hath willed
> His truth to triumph through us.
> Our ancient vicious foe
> Still seeks to work his woe.
> His craft and power are great
> And armed with cruel hate,
> Our earth is not his equal.

Luther's continual bouts with Satan, who often came personally to annoy him, lent credibility to the Devil's existence among Luther's followers, as it also did among those who saw Luther himself as Satan's tool. If God and Catholicism suffered during those troubled times, Satan revelled, for he alone emerged unscathed and, far from being altered or weakened, stronger than ever before.

Satan's prominence, his fiendish cleverness, was so great that in the year 1474 at Basle proof that he even extended his malevolence to animals came to light when a chicken with the plumage and bearing of a rooster laid an egg, to the horror of churchmen and laymen alike. A proper court was convened, the rooster was formally charged as being in league with the Devil, and was condemned to be burned at the stake, which sentence was carried out before an assembly of solemn spectators.

In the year 1270 an abbot, Richalmus, noted that when he had over-eaten; demons made him feel uncomfortable, and when he put a hand inside his vestments, devils "tickle[d] and bit it like fleas"; when his clothing rustled as Abbot Richalmus moved, devils spoke to him "through this sound".

Additional aid to Satan came through a unique legal case in which Satan versus Christ captured the common imagination of medieval Christians. Satan lost the lawsuit, but acquitted himself well through his advocates.

The learned and devout author of *Dialogus Miraculorum*, Caesarius von Heisterbach, in his text for young monks, noted in all seriousness that Satan once appeared to a confessor, and after enumerating his sins, was told by the sceptical priest that no one could have done all those wicked things in less than 1,000 years. Satan admitted that he was indeed, a good bit older than 1,000 years. The priest then asked if Satan desired to do penance, and, upon being told by Satan that he might consider it, the priest said that Satan must "bow down thrice a day, saying: 'God, my Lord and Creator, I have sinned against thee, forgive me.'" Satan refused. "No," he told the priest, "that would be too humiliating for me."

Centuries before the Reformation the intrigues of man as well as the blinding virtue of God, or gods, would have served no purpose at all without Satan. Salvation, redemption, even perhaps re-birth itself, would have had no significance. But by the sixteenth century, when the common view—at least of Protestants— was that a debased Catholicism served Satan as well, and at times even better, than it served God; Satan thrived as never before and as he never thrived again, although this period, of necessity no longer referred to as the Reformation by the seventeenth and early eighteenth centuries, continued to echo the earlier changes and implications, all to the glory of not God but Satan.

Catholicism's duly appointed 'Devil's Advocate', was in fact not Satan's servant but the Church's. His duty was to derogate, with valid proof, those commended for Catholic honorariums, such as saints and heroes, the idea evidently being that if he could prevent sainthood from being conferred he would thus deprive Heaven of a worthy candidate, and presumably in this manner deprive the Lord of a supporter. But the Devil's Advocate in this instance did not actually promote satanism, nor even actually augment the legions of Hell; the fact that he might prevent a devout from achieving canonization did not mean the devout went to Hell, it simply meant that his—or her—qualifications were inadequate for beatification or whatever.

The genuine advocates of Satan were men such as Constantine the Great, Simon Magus and Thomas Aquinas, who, through either their unique personal aberrations, or through their zealous logic, brought forth both the Reformation and the Holy Inquisition, in both of which Satan figured very prominently. Satan was confirmed in stature by Christians; those who most opposed him did him the greatest honour. Legitimate miracles, rare in the Church, were the workings of God, all else was necromancy, witchcraft, black magic, the work of Satan, and it was this latter variety of miracle that was most common. When it was said that a miracle had occurred, and priests at once denied the evidence, then palpably—since an unusual event had been witnessed, had in fact taken place despite denial—if it could *not* be the workings of God it *had* to be the working of the Devil.

It did not help the image of Christianity's Jesus that many miracles mentioned in the Apocrypha were both cruel and criminal, but this did not necessarily reflect upon Satan. His 'miracles' were more common and, in consequence of ecclesiastical disassociation, could be said without fear of contradiction to be specifically and categorically his alone.

One of the greatest theologians of the Reformation, Henricus Cornelius Agrippa AB Nettesheim, in his *De Occulta Philosophia* (1531) stated it as his conviction that through "celestial" magic, meaning true illumination or union with divinity, men could cast spells, including evil and wicked ones, and work contra-natural phenomenon.

He worked out an elaborate philosophy in which science, mathematics and mysticism all figured. After years of experimentation, most notable for consistent failures, he decided that there could be no such thing as science; and in 1526, nine years before his death, Agrippa wrote the book that reflected his disillusionment, and that had such a profound affect on many devouts who had thought of Agrippa as an 'illuminated' and therefore infallible Christian.

Any disillusionment by a Church leader had to reflect against, not just the Church, but against Christianity; and, through inadvertence, it had conversely to strengthen the power of Satan through fear.

This same fact held true during the shameful epoch of witch persecution. The fact that the Church was so merciless in its persecution inevitably forced people to wonder if in times of travail, as when Saul visited the Witch of Endor, appealing to Satan might not expedite succour. The Church itself related the most astounding tales of satanic magic and miracles. Disillusionment with the Church, the Pope, with God's word itself, not only reflected against the entire Christian cosmogony, it also encouraged a leaning towards that other power, the one even the Church declared was powerful.

Satan was never busier than during the Reformation and for the several ensuing centuries; his devils had never before been so well authenticated, nor so well received.

When the Church came out in wrath against Satan as the giver of illicit power, wealth, even happiness, there could not have been a greater encouragement for the destitute, the weak and defence-less, the poverty-ridden and hopeless, to turn to Satan for that which, if he could indeed supply it, had certainly never been sup-plied by Christianity, its powerful popes or its martyred Saviour. Therefore, too, the Church was Satan's advocate.

Even when thousands were tortured, broken and burned as heretics, as witches; as fearful as that punishment was, fighting for food with scavenging dogs in Europe's alleys was little better. If all Satan required was a soul, there were millions willing to barter souls in exchange for alleviation; or, if they did not know hunger or terminal disease and wanted power instead of peace, they would still barter.

The Church further strengthened Satan when its refused to sanction 'good' magic as opposed to evil or 'black' magic. During the ages of almost total ignorance about illness and disease, magic spells designed to aid or cure ailments (good or 'white' magic) were denounced right along with 'black' or satanic magic. Many people, some of whom actually caused cures with herbs and a 'laying on of hands' were put to death for serving Satan through the heresy of magic. A surgeon who managed to save the life of a newborn child in Hamburg, Germany, in the year 1521, was put to death for practising black magic.

The Christian ritual was magic. Poor magic, to be sure, for the elaborately attired magicians—priests—who performed expiatory and sacramental magic ritual at their altars rarely managed to accomplish much. Still, the entire panoply was magic pure and simple. The difference, when one existed, was claimed by the Church to be the difference between *Church* magic, which obtained with God's blessing, and *black* magic, which throve on Satan's sanction.

The Church did not deny that Satan could be worshipped. It said, on the contrary, that Satanists parodied God's ritual in most shocking and obscene ways, and that the Devil himself often attended these frightful affairs. Satan was not scorned—which would have injured him; instead, he was eulogized in the most serious and hair-raising manner.

Strict admonition against associating with wicked people, witches and black magicians, implied that such people knew of things that might gratify Christians. There was no surer temptation. Those few men who, even before the Reformation, scoffed at a Devil who appeared on earth, were the ones who were scorned. The Church, clearly at war with Hell, was the best imaginable evidence that Satan was not a myth. Church denunciation was official recognition that the Devil *was* real, that he came among men, and had a power that very often rivalled God's power, and certainly, since it was derived from supernaturalism, exceeded Church power. What possible additional evidence proving Satan's reality could be offered?

For centuries the Church concentrated on perfecting counter-magic. As early as the eighth and ninth centuries, when converts were baptized, this ceremony was performed solely to exorcize evil spirits. All Christian sacraments were magic rituals analogous to exorcism. The Church was an institution of ritual sorcery from top to bottom, not very different in purpose from the old-time theologies, and yet it condemned with zealous fury and savagery the same, or only slightly varied, rituals in other faiths, and even among its own sects. Heresy was any kind of worship that differed from Church worship. It was the Devil's work, and for many centuries Church persecution encouraged a very real fear of Catholicism while it is also occasioned an almost unquestioned belief in the Devil as an individual of enormous power and cunning—not in an abstract sense but as a rival of God, with a vast subterranean hierarchy.

Church power reached for and cowed such scoffers as Galileo, Huss, Giordano Bruno, and the noted Dominican, Savonarola, who was excommunicated, broken at torture, and burned to the Glory of God!

If, as some churchmen claimed, the Devil could bring down such men as these, his power was indeed very respectable. Each time such a man of worth or substance was revealed as a heretic, a minion of Satan, a leaguer of Hell, people whose existence, as well as their knowledge, was liable to insecurity and ignorance, could be expected to accept as fact the existence of that evil power.

There never were better advocates of Satan than those who professed to hate and fear him the most. Nor was there ever a less perceptive company of lords than the popes of Rome from the era of Leo the Great to Clement XIV—with a few exceptions. In the matter of Satan versus humanity, they consistently averred the power and existence of an entity that one Roman reign based on ridicule could have banished throughout Christendom; and not one of those Lords of the Church had either the perception, or the courage, to kill Satan in the only way he could have been slain—by neglect, derision, ridicule. Thus those God-serving popes did as good a job at Satan-serving.

TWELVE

Atheists, Pagans and Satan

The darkest era in the history of Hell under Christian sponsorship occurred when all sectarians who failed in their convictions to equate with the lofty aims of Rome's Mother Church were denounced as heretics and adherents of Satan.

During this lengthy and bitter period Hell's hierarchy was able to expand until, according to theologians, there were no less than thirteen separate diabolical orders. Some Churchmen claimed the number was closer to twenty, and other learned men increased the number rather significantly by including, not only the thirteen individual orders *in* Hell, but all *earthly* non-conformist faiths, including Montanists, Navatian Puritans, as well as the Albigenses and those sects the Church had already moved against with the sword and stake.

In Germany when the Bishop of Bremen used force to collect tithes and an uprising ensued, it was put down with unprecedented savagery and slaughter on the grounds that the people who had resisted had obviously done so because, as Satanists, they chose not to give money that the Church would use to the Glory of God.

The Church, it was noted, existed surrounded by Satanists, mostly witches who had learned the black rituals from devils. There were even devils within the Church. Satan's legions were everywhere by day as well as by night; they worked zealously to augment by all means the forces arrayed against God and the Pope.

But the underlying conviction of Satanism, supported by Luther and others, came out of the Reformation unshaken; and Protestants joined Catholics in committing the same enormities, but for a different reason. The very Protestants held by Rome to be heretics, allies of Satan, in turn persecuted other deviants who were thought to be diabolists—not because Protestants considered these people as anti-clerical heretics, but because, for three centuries, everyone was convinced Satan was recruiting mortals. Among *all* Christians, anyone, even devout churchmen, who could possibly be accused, were liable to prosecution as diabolists.

There was not much difference, in the devout view, between a wizard, a witch, a satanist or a heretic. Ecclesiastical logic followed the edict of Deuteronomy: all dreamers of dreams, prophets, givers of signs shall be put to death.

The definitions, heathen, pagan, athiest, heretic, were used interchangeably. Pagans were initially country people, those who believed in sylphs, fairies, woodland, lake, fen and mountain, spirits. The Church called them heathens, idolators, worshippers of false gods and carried on an unrelenting campaign of extermination against them.

In former times a pagan was simply a rural village dweller (Latin: *pagus* meaning country, *paganus* meaning a countryman, a villager.) In Roman times the *paganalia*, or annual rural festival, was common, and of course the polytheism of Rome had a prominent place in these celebrations. Hence it was possible for Christians to view those affairs of pagans, or countrymen, as an abomination. Pagans became heathens, heretics, vile idolators; and in time the term was broadened by churchmen to include absolute materialists, people lacking religion of any kind, and people, religious or otherwise, who lacked ethics.

To be accused as a pagan was the same as being denounced as an atheist, but only after the fullness of time and zealous frenzy of the Holy Office blurred distinctions to this extent, because atheism in its basic concept was a disbelief in, or a denial of, the existence of God, and pagans were anything but non-believers. As a rule they recognized an entire catalogue of gods. Also, there was the contra-distinction among Christian agnostics who did not deny God; they simply disclaimed knowledge of Him.

But pagans, atheists, agnostics, heathens, idolators, regardless of the designation, were held to be heretics, the most vile and debased of mortal men. According to orthodox theological doctrine in earlier times, even Christians were called atheists because they denied the divinity of Roman and Greek gods. Later, the exact opposite view predominated when Christianity had grown strong.

Practical atheism flourished in every highly developed civilization. In later ages both India and China were atheistic in their systems of Jainism and Buddhism. Inevitably, a vigorous materialism encourages atheism. The materialism of classical antiquity found expression in the Atomists, Democritus, Epicurus and Lucretius. (It was Lucretius who held that the greatest single disaster ever to befall mankind, was religion.)

The atheism of the eighteenth century found an outlet in the teachings of La Mettrie, D'Holbach, Diderot and Vogt. Still later, Hackel and Compte advanced theories that were atheistic in essence since they attempted to explain the universe without reference to any divine being.

Church custom and precedent did not support debate with pagans or atheists, on the grounds that heresy did not deserve recognition, but rather extermination. A heretic by any definition was fundamentally a servant of Satan. The course was clear, Deuteronomy was explicit: Any people whose gods were different were blasphemers; "Thou shalt not consent unto him nor harken unto him; neither shall thine eye pity him, neither shall thou spare, neither shalt thou conceal him: But thou shalt surely kill him; thine hand shall be first upon him to put him to death. . . . And thou shalt stone him with stones, that he die. . . ."

Non-believers "from one end of the earth even unto the other end of the earth" were subject to this dictum. If they failed to acknowledge Catholic Christianity they were pagans and aethists, the most abominable people on earth, and deserved death without quarter. St. Jerome (340–420) advocated death to them all, as did Pope Leo the Great (440–461). Pope Alexander III was as zealous as were Innocent III and his predecessor Gregory VII whose fanatacism and militancy humbled Philip Augustus of France, broke Emperor Otto IV, and forced King John of England to acknowledge the feudal supremacy of the Pope; and each of these great lords of the Church carried their unyielding obduracy against atheists, infidels and pagans—all alleged satanists—to such extremes that no one was safe. Innocent III inaugurated the fourth Crusade in his zeal to crush heretics, deviants, and unclean infidels, all servants of Satan.

Gregory IX established the Holy Office for the express purpose of rooting out individual satanists in Italy in the year 1224. The Council of Toulouse in 1229 confirmed Gregory's policy, and subsequently the dark age of holy murder grew and spread, its purpose nothing less than a ritual war against the Devil. In the year 1232 Pope Gregory formed the Order of Dominicans; as papal inquisitors they were charged with seeking for torture and death every suspected heretic. So pitiless and cruel were these monks that they came to be known as *Domini canes*, 'the sleuth-hounds of the Lord'.

Again it was claimed that Satan was in retreat; but when Gregory sent an empowered representative, Conrad of Marburg, to Germany to establish a Holy Office, Satan struck back. After indicating, among others of high station, Count Henry of Sayn, for heresy, Conrad was overtaken on the road leading to Paderborn by several irate German knights, and on 30th July 1233 was put to the sword. Pope Gregory canonized him and commanded that a chapel be erected on the spot where Conrad had been slain; and eventually, although there was sporadic resistence throughout Germany for years to come, the Holy Office took root there.

In France the imps of Hell had become so numerous, had converted so many people, that the jails, donjons, and torture chambers could not hold them all, and Charles IV had a mammoth prison built expressly to accommodate these vile and debased human beings. It was called the Bastille.

Atheism was widespread and acknowledgement of this fact was rarely disputed; but of all those most learned and devout zealots who insisted on killing everyone accused as a heretic, and who so feared the power of Hell, not one came forward to state as a fact that for every Satanist burned and sent to Hell the Devil's legions were inevitably increased by one; nor was it ever advocated that perhaps through divine mercy the pagans and atheists might be saved on earth—an accomplishment that might, conceivably, not only have deprived Hell of a resident, but might more advantageously have supplied Heaven with an angel.

Salvation did not necessarily embody compromise; the function of priests was to harvest converts, and the field was singularly open to them; but Church policy actually discouraged both conversion and salvation. Pope Innocent III, who exacted such bloody retribution from the Albigenses, enjoined all churchmen, upon pain of severe punishment for disobedience, to seek out and prosecute without fail and without mercy, all who dared worship in ways that differed in even the slightest degree from the methods of Rome.

The wicked atheists and pagans accomplished one noteable feat: they served as the basis for Church unity. When it was claimed that Hell's devils were coming to earth by the hundreds and tens of hundreds, an embattled Church wasted little time in forming a solid rank of ecclesiastics to battle Satan and his legions. The Church also broadened its political base, for no other reason, obviously, than to carry on its war with the Lord of Darkness. In this way, as spiritual leaders of Christendom, the popes were able to establish supremacy over temporal kings and emperors. The heretics had presented the Church with its greatest opportunity to confirm the Vatican's power over *all* men, to the Glory of God; and, like all power, once it was established by force it had to be overthrown by force.

The Catholic policy of taking advantage of all opportunities obtained during the centuries of the Satan-mania. Every pope who ruled from the Vatican during those generations used the Satan-mania and the fear it inspired as a means for strengthening the Church. When it appeared that belief in Satan's strength might lag, Church edicts and zealotry aroused it anew. Satan was Catholicism's great supporter, exactly as Christ was Catholicism's great reason. Caught between were atheists, pagans, heretics of many kinds who, because they heard different trumpets, were the foe for whom there could be neither mercy nor salvation.

Eventually, in the year 1404, the Synod of Langres offered a note of hope: all Satanists who would confess, repent, and do penance, might hope for salvation. However, to confess was risky and to offer to do penance was no guarantee that fasts and fines and pilgrimages would automatically ensue. The number of confessed witches and diabolists burned and tortured to death was greatest in some areas of Europe during the fifteenth century; and devils who were exorcized during that period told harrowing tales of Hell on the march. It was during the residency of Pope Eugene (1431–47) that inquisitors were instructed by circular letter to hunt down and destroy heretics "summarily, without ado, and

without any judiciary form". Thus the olive branch extended by
the Synod of Langres could be and undoubtedly was, in some
areas, considered not as a benign act, but as a sly means of
encouraging Satanists to come forth and repent so that the Church
could scourge them.

The chances for heretics to elude Church vengeance were not
very good even prior to the establishment of the Holy Office; but
after its establishment there was no chance at all. In some
Catholic lands a bounty was offered those willing to help in God's
work. In nations such as Spain where the Directorium Inquisi-
torium of Eymerich, Inquisitor-General of Castile and predecessor of the infamous yet paradoxical Torquemada, was organized
as though the war with Satan were an actual armed conflict.
There were spies, a spoils system, bounties offered to traitors,
rewards for valour, and armed hosts ready to fight by day or
night.

Superstitious peasants in Spain, France, the Lowlands, Germany (*Catholic* Germany), Italy, even in those parts of Scandinavia where popes were honoured, had no recourse and were permitted no defence against a charge of heresy. But not only
peasants suffered. No less a great lord than Archbishop Carranza,
primate of the Church of Spain, was accused by the Holy Office.

It was very probable that peasants were pagans—rarely
atheists, though, rural people have always been superstitious—
and it was just as conceivable that lords and great warriors were
genuine atheists; but when the charge of heresy was made the
specific definition, or the suspected degree of wickedness, was
unimportant. Those who were arraigned were accused of devia-
tion, of straying from Church ritual and edict—unpardonable
heresy—and from that one charge, regardless of whatever else
might have been involved, there was no pardon. On this basis it
was possible to accuse, try, condemn, and burn, such an exalted
leader—*church* leader—as Archbishop Carranza. Whatever devia-
tion he had dared, Satan made him do it. Punishment was as
natural a result as breathing.

It was Satan, infiltrating even the chaste order of Knights
Templars, causing debasement, that aroused the Church to
denounce that fraternity. It was Satan's imps who infiltrated the
Rosicrucian Order in the Middle Ages, encouraging perverted

sexuality and priapic rites, that brought the Church out against members of the Order of the Rose Cross. And much later, in the year 1739 when Church power was no longer as great, although the zealotry was unabated, a pope denounced Freemasons, who had obviously been infiltrated by devils from Hell, because not only did Freemasons engage in secret rites, but they did so while accepting both Catholics and heretical Protestants into their membership.

No one suggested to inquisitors or popes, nor to Protestant witch-hunters and anti-satanists, that of all men those least likely to believe in Satan and Hell were those same atheists who did not believe in God or Heaven, either.

If a man failed to acknowledge an orderly cosmogony based on the principle of good, then obviously it was unlikely that he believed in any such fantasy as organized evil, and that being true, an atheist was not a Satanist; he could not be one since he did not believe there were gods, good *or* evil.

But in the Church view—in the view of *both* churches, Catholic and Protestant—atheism was anathema, not only because it was heretical, a denunciation of God, but also because atheism was a very great threat to religion—greater in fact, than the differences between faiths or sects, for an atheist scoffed at *all* religion, and that was a dangerous kind of man, or dogma, to leave unburied.

Satan would welcome pagans into Hell, but one is entitled to doubt that an atheist ever arrived there. Still, while this might be a rational view, it most certainly was no such thing during those bloody centuries when Christianity abetted Satan by killing hundreds of thousands of its own people and sending them below. In those generations there was very little rationality; no one ever raised the question of atheists being the most improbable of Satanists for the basic reason that inquisitors were in search of victims, not seeking reasons why people could *not* be victims.

There was another aspect of persecution that managed to elude the ecclesiastics. While people possessed by devils, or those who had sold their souls to devils, or others who were Satanists through intimation or allegation, were burned by the hundreds of thousands; all this inward, psychotic genocide did nothing towards eliminating devils, it only succeeded in killing duped or deluded human beings. So, what the Church actually accomplished in its centuries-old war with Satan, was to deliberately kill its own troops.

All those great minds of the Reformation and earlier, all such sainted and hallowed men as Thomas Aquinas, never conceived of a way to destroy devils; only one another. This had to be Satan's greatest triumph, and it was an obvious one; 1,000 years after the hierarchy of Hell was publicized, the same lords, demons, wights, imps and fiends were carried on the rosters. Thousands of human beings had been put to death, but no sooner was one victim roasted to ashes than his possessing devil turned up somewhere else, inhabiting another human victim; and although everyone of whatever affiliation, secular or ecclesiastical, knew who the real foe was, no one ever successfully devised a way to kill devils.

For the pagan with his droll nature spirits or the atheist who lacked even these companions, Christianity's madness must have appeared as unprecedented as it was deadly. If this sentiment obtained—and it most certainly did among many people subsequent to the advent of Christ, a fact attested by Church records—it is possible that in proportion to those hundreds of thousands of Christians put to death on suspicion, the number of executed pagans and atheists must have been infinitesimal. These people, while doubtless repelled by Christianity, were also made very wary and prudent by it.

THIRTEEN

Satan Worship

Although there can be little doubt that earlier man observed propitiatory celebrations favouring evil by whatever name he chose to designate it, he no more worshipped Satan than did his European descendants. He feared evil in so many forms a dozen polytheisms sprang up around it; and while he built temples offered sacrifices—frequently human—wore amulets and burnt incense in recognition of evil, these were not forms of worship, they were varieties of placating obeisance.

There was good reason. Hail, cloudbursts, fire, tempests, plagues, darkness, illness, invasion, lightning, misadventures, injuries, drought, hunger, cold, every discomfort that could trouble earliest man, was very serious to him, and because he knew of no particular reason why many of these things happened, he assumed they occurred because a wicked spirit or god made them happen for some personal reason, or simply because wicked gods disliked human beings.

In later centuries sorcerers were said to be Devil-worshippers, but again, even the witches who presumably participated in Black Masses at Sabbats worshipped Satan less than they served him in exchange for a favour, or for several favours. It was a *pact*, not a faith, these people demonstrated.

The abominations said to have taken place at medieval Sabbats—such as reciting prayers and instituting Satan's name where God's name was normally used; defiling the cross, the Sacrament, church altars, and so forth—were acts of defiance against God (usually Catholicism rather than the actual Trinity or Divinity), not acts of reverence for Satan. But the Church viewed all of these acts as antichristian. This they were if one adopted a Catholic view that everything was heresy that did not originate in Christianity; but Antichrist was not necessarily, or even commonly, pro-Satan.

Satan might have re-emerged as a god worthy of temples and rituals, amulets and obeisances, because when the Church defined Hell it made that place indescribably worse than any previous Hell; but the Church adopted and renovated a fairly common old legend of an in-between-place, named it Purgatory, and for centuries both Satan and Hell suffered.

Purgatory was a place of discomfort but it was nowhere nearly as frightful as Hell. Moreover, souls could expect reinstatement, after suitable expiation and punishment, from Purgatory. 'Hell everlasting' had no such convenient limitation on penance.

Purgatory came in time to fairly well replace Hell among Catholics. The Church's description of Hell and eternal damnation was so hair-raising that as time passed almost no one accepted Hell as an ultimate destination regardless of their wickedness; but everyone during the Middle Ages was entirely satisfied with the concept of Purgatory, or limited punishment for evil-doers.

Prior to the advent of Dante, Christian writers depicted Hell only rarely, although both writers and artists depicted Purgatory very often. In fact, churchmen appeared to favour Purgatory over Hell so often that it is probably correct to say that during the Middle Ages, although men might be certain their enemies would go to Hell, they did not believe they, themselves, would go there, and they had ecclesiastical assurance that this was true. Penances often had less to do with saving the soul from Hell than they had to do with shortening the length of time an evil-doer had to spend in Purgatory, and the result of this was that Satan and his hierarchy were not as feared as early Christian prelates had hoped they might be by those inclined towards wickedness but afraid of its consequences.

Next to derision or the fatal curse of neglect, Satan suffered most from the concept of an in-between-place, for the souls sent there were not within his grasp, and could achieve redemption, something they had no hope of achieving once they went to Hell.

But this same belief that Purgatory, as a place of temporary abode for evil-doers, and from which it was possible to be saved, was the more likely destination of the dead, also seemed to encourage a good many people to flirt with Satan. It was a common belief in medieval times, and the Church certainly encouraged it, that once an evil act was perpetrated, penance with a view towards Church indulgence, or seeking redemption through genuine repentance, could save the penitent from Hell, if not from a sojourn in Purgatory. On these grounds many people were willing to consort with devils, and the objective was to acquire health, wealth, happiness or power through satanic assistance, but without giving up the soul in exchange.

Early magic rituals had a large number of incantations and secret rites calling up devils to aid a supplicant in acquiring whatever it was his heart desired; and an integral part of these rites was some defensive or protective charm, such as speaking aloud the name of Jesus Christ, thought to have a power for making demons slink back to Hell, which was to be used if the wily devil appeared to be on the verge of entrapping the supplicant into yielding up his soul. The idea was that as long as a man retained his soul he was eligible for Purgatory, but once he succumbed and surrendered his soul to a devil, when he died he most certainly would go to Hell. This was in large part at the root of all convictions concerning Satan's desire for souls, just as it also was the basis for Christianity's passion for saving them.

But these people who invoked devils were not devil-worshippers. At the worst, as in Faust's example and that of a few others who allegedly actually contacted devils, they were out-smarted by demons; while at the best, they managed to secure riches or power through a diabolic influence, but kept their souls, and were therefore eligible for Purgatory and eventual redemption, being fortunate enough, or clever enough, to have the best of both worlds. Whatever the result of their strategy, they did not worship Satan. Obeisance, propitiation, even homage, did not amount to worship. Fear had little in common with adoration. The black alters used in diabolic rites had nothing in common with Church altars, except the dimensions.

There *have* been sects favouring Satan, but they belonged to places such as Africa; and generally these worshippers were involved with a black spirit that was both good *and* evil. He did not possess the totally evil and malicious character of Christianity's Satan, but, like all gods men have favoured, could and often did, cause the crops, the kine, and the fecundity of women, to prosper—things Christianity's devils could not do, being completely and whole-heartedly dedicated to wickedness.

During the centuries of witch-persecution in Europe and, to a lesser degree, in America, it was mandatory at arraignments for the alleged witch or wizard to be accused of worshipping the Devil. A defence was never offered that claimed the accused were only trying to deceive or use Satan, but had such a defence been made, of course it could not have saved a victim from torture and the stake, because in the common view anyone who even *thought* of Satan was contaminated. So it was that those thousands of unfortunates who were put to death as Devil-worshippers were guilty of heresy by implication, by suggestion, and not at all by fact.

Any number of transcripts are extant detailing the outcries of victims under torture who, usually at first, denounced Satan and called on Christ to succour them, but only a rare few continued to deny that they worshipped Satan and had forsaken Jesus; with broken bodies, deranged minds, or while still rational enough to accept the torturer's suggestion, most victims confessed to adoring the Devil. But this scarcely constituted proof; instead, it was an agonized human being's acceptance of a simple fact: if an agreement, a confession, was necessary to escape further torture, then it was best to admit to a lie.

In his book *The History Of The Devil*, Dr. Paul Carus says that "Demonaltry, or Devil-worship, is the first stage in the evolution of religion . . .", which refers to *fear* as the basis of religion; yet this kind of religion is not faith, and it most certainly is not adoration. A fearful worshipper does not seek oneness with his god, he seeks only to placate him, which in fact is exactly what primitive man sought to do; and while it would be imprudent to deny that the first theologies were not based on fear of evil, the principle involved was not religion, it was dread. There is a corollary, obviously, but one in which faith, conviction, salvation, the essences of true religion, had no part; therefore what Dr. Carus referred to was not religion at all, it was superstition. His

Devil-worshippers did not venerate Satan, they were simply afraid not to try and placate him.

It has been the custom for years to say that those who offered human sacrifices were Devil-worshippers. The evil deity of early Mexico, Huitzilopochtli, in whose stone temples human victims were slain in propitiatory rites, was not *the* god of Mexicans; he was their Devil. They sacrificed to him to ward off evil, not because they venerated him, and when the King of Moab submitted his son as an immolated offering (2 Kings, iii, 27), the purpose was to placate not venerate. Even when Jeptha believed God required that he sacrifice his daughter by burning (Judges, xi, 29–40), although outraged chroniclers denounced Jeptha as a servant of Satan, the fact was that Jeptha was the Devil's foe.

When Euripedes recorded the sacrifice of Polyxena on the tomb of Achilles to pacify the Greek hero's spirit and assure a safe return of the Greek army, although subsequent scholars and historians called this a form of Satan-worship by heathens, the Greek pantheon was far from Devil-oriented. Sacrifices were common in all ages when life was cheap. Satan to the Greeks was not holy, and it would be wide of the fact to say the Greeks were Devil-worshippers.

The error appears to be largely a matter of definition, of semantics. When it is written that "Religion always begins with fear... the fear of evil and the various efforts made to escape evil," the mistake is a common one. What *should* be said is that "*Superstition* always begins with fear, etc. ...." Further, when the generic term *god* is used, the difficulty is compounded. For example, set, or Seth, the evil demon of death, is called "a strong god whose anger is to be feared". But Seth was a *devil*. When it was written that the Egyptians worshipped a "god called Seth" what was meant was that the Egyptians propitiated a devil named Seth; but because in the old pantheons all supernatural beings were designated as gods whether good or evil, meaning simply that they were supernatural, when the monotheists, the believers in *one god*, came on the scene, ignorance or intolerance—probably more of the latter—enabled them to claim that the Egyptians were Devil-worshippers.

Dr. Carus, previously cited, noted that "until the positive power of good is recognized and man finds out by experience that the good, although its power may be ever so slow, is always victorious in the end . . . then the power of evil [will] cease . . . to be an object of awe."

The fallacy seems to be that good is *not* always victorious in the end, and that man will never cease to be awed (influenced) by evil. Hitler wasn't and neither was Stalin, nor will other men, because evil is as essential to God as it is to man. Without it men would have very little reason to seek the perfection they attribute to God's will.

Those in former times who came closest to venerating Satan belonged to the theologies who saw in God both good and evil. This duality, which has been prevalent in so many of the great religions but particularly in the monotheistic ones, enabled worshippers who could not ignore the presence of evil, to rationalize its existence into an acceptable and understandable form, and still believe God was superior to Satan, by reasoning that God allowed Satan and evil to exist.

Under Christianity God's power became greater than Satan's power, an inevitable result of monotheism. But at the same time as this happened, more evil appeared in the world than had ever appeared before, an embarrassing corollary unless the Christians could reasonably explain this phenomenon and still not admit that their God was incapable of controlling evil.

This same corollary had appeared many times before, so the Christians, as they so frequently did, could refer to the explanations of others—pagans, heathens, idolators—and bring forth the same contention, which they did by saying in essence that God allowed Satan to tempt men in order to make his adherents strong in the faith—another way of saying that God allowed evil to exist, or, as troubled prehistoric men believed, that a king of kings, a lord of gods, was both good *and* evil; was both God *and* Satan.

It has always been logical to respect a strong enemy. The monotheists had this fact thrust upon them as soon as they did away with all the lesser gods, yet still had Hell on their hands. They had no alternative than to maintain that their God knew

Satan and suffered him. They also had to make veneration of their God the only way for Christians to find salvation; and gradually, over the centuries, God's tolerance of evil was relegated a minor part in the faith because, patently, it aroused more questions and more scepticism than it resolved.

God under the Christian theology, was good, was deserving of veneration and adoration. Satan under the Christian dogma, deserved respect. There were propitiatory rites but these were never confused, at least among knowledgeable Christians, with worship. Neither were they viewed in that light by earlier devouts —unless the devout at prayer could separate the evil from the good, and of course that has never been possible except in a personal, individual, completely selfish context.

In any case, there has never been a general nor total veneration of evil of the kind implied by the use of such a term as Devil-worship. The reason this has not obtained is simply because man, whether in the prehistoric life-experience or in any of the later or relatively recent life-experiences, never co-existed with total evil. Historically, there have been two variations of the religious theme; good—bad and indifferent. Agnostics chose the latter, the negativism of simply not knowing. All others have chosen a compromise that included prevalent and obvious evil, and consistent, pleasurable good; but in neither case was the Devil exclusively venerated.

Impersonal detachment has never been a virtue devouts, secular or ecclesiastical, could develop or, apparently, tolerate—otherwise the warped zealotry of popes, saints, patristics and other fanatics would have avoided both the condemnation and the condescension, the uncompromising anathema so particularly noticeable among the early Mohammedans, Jews and Christians, which allowed them in their righteous indignation to classify all nonbelievers as infidels and Devil-worshippers.

It is from these men that such an incorrect term derived, and later, it was easier to follow their example than to suspect it, so the definition passed into the history, as well as the theologies of man, perpetuating its falsity.

Satan benefited. He was made great by this wrong assumption, so great in fact that thousands of people who had no knowledge

(left) King Solomon with his wives at table, from *The Reliquary and Shrine of the True Riches of Salvation and Eternal Blessedness*, 1491. (right) "Merlin and Vivien" by Sir Edward Burne-Jones

"The Fall of the Rebel Angels" by Hieronymus Bosch

of Devil-worship were put to death on the assumption that they practised it.

Ecclesiastics filled entire libraries and spent whole lifetimes proving that people worshipped Satan. They influenced ten generations of otherwise more or less rational human beings, in Christendom alone, to believe this monumental fallacy. At the same time they venerated a God that, unless they also admitted had to be responsible for the existence of wickedness, was impaired by each instance they used as an example to prove how powerful Satan was.

The great hoax of witchcraft, which was as uniquely Christian as it was incapable of being catalogued as mythology, folklore, or anthropology, but which lay in the exclusive province of theology, arose from the concept of Devil-worship; and in Christendom was found the epitome of this belief, which, despite its longevity, was fallacious from beginning to end. It was also, incidentally, the most savage and depraved example of mass murder Christianity ever inaugurated among its own adherents. All to the glory of the Devil.

Those gloomy devout who imagined the black rites of Devil-worship throughout Europe created an entire black theology based on their knowledge of Christian dogma and ritual—and no one ever accused them of perpetuating the most unforgivable of all heresies—yet in fact this is exactly what they did.

Their books were full of sexuality, always perverted, orgiastically bestial, and of course reflecting the psychotic imbalance imposed by their own unhealthy celibacy. These churchmen who so fiercely denounced the Greeks for offering up human sacrifices did the exact same thing by demanding an identical immolation of heretics at the stake.

They did less, by far, to perpetuate the divinity of Christianity's God, than they did to strengthen Christianity's Satan, and they did it so well that, from the closing decade of their bloody persecution of alleged Devil-worshippers to the present time, Christianity by a tacit agreement which has been reflected in lowered church attendance as well by the mushrooming of schismatic sects, has steadily declined.

God remains, of course, and so does Satan; but while modern

H

man refuses to accept Satan as anything more than an abstraction, not as Martin Luther's grinning physical entity, so does modern man view God as a variety of unknowable, baffling, logarithm of some kind. The Church that exalted both, never succeeded in killing Satan; but it came awfully close to killing God in its maniacal preoccupation with the myth of Devil-worshippers.

FOURTEEN

Invocations

Before an invocation could be successfully undertaken, one elemental conception had to be honestly acknowledged: if God was a symbol or an allegory signifying an actual presence, then the idea of the Devil also represented a reality. In other words, it could do no good to go through an invocation calling forth a devil if the supplicant did not honestly believe there were devils, any more than praying to God could accomplish anything if a supplicant did not conceive of God as an involved and responsive intelligence.

Undoubtedly the majority of people from early until recent times believed the Devil was as real as God also was, and since those people believed in angels they could just as readily believe in demons. In fact prior to the Reformation, during that period, and subsequently, when the schism was still fresh and meaningful, it was easier in those troubled times to imagine demons than it was to fantasize angels.

Innumerable accounts of devils on earth existed, but there were very few explanations that detailed the actual procession involved in how they got there. An idea prevailed that devils either appeared voluntarily, or they were somehow invoked. Aside from Johann Faust, who was suspect even during his own lifetime, a few notables such as Roger Bacon were thought capable of invoking them.

Meaner spirits, some who possessed people, the imps of Hell, a very low order of malevolent but generally trivial entities, were thought to always be around, lurking in dark places, caves, lakes, treetops, under large stones; and commonly they gained access to human beings in a very reasonable way. They hid in the grass which cattle ate, then they hid inside the cattle until the animals were butchered, and passed into human beings who ate the meat. This kind of devil, however, was associated more with aching joints and upset stomachs than with genuine wickedness. They could not motivate their victims, for example, to commit murder or blasphemy, they could only cause discomfort. Illness was attributable to them, miscarriages, toothache, sundry physical discomforts; and their external manifestations were such forms as ringworm, an assortment of venereal diseases, or perhaps a ravenous and sudden gluttony. But these were common blights and as a rule they did not cause death—at least not quickly nor suddenly—and their influence rarely extended beyond the possessed person.

Otherwise, these wights or imps could be exorcized. Churchmen quite often managed to rid some possessed wretch of his devil by ordering those suffering from stomach pains to drink milk every day before praying; or those in whose feet imps dwelt, to put their feet into hot water twice a day and keep them there throughout the telling of a rosary.

Exorcizing the higher order of devils was another matter. It was only rarely successful, but at issue was how devils of those higher orders came to earth, how they happened to serve individual people, and why they caused death, degradation, dishonour, to other people.

It was never assumed that demons of the more exalted orders appeared among mortals simply for the hell of it. These were reasoning, correctly motivated entities; like prosperous merchants they did nothing just because an impulse prompted them to do it. Therefore it was not assumed that they appeared on earth unless they had been properly invoked.

A noted treatise previously mentioned, *The Clavicle of Solomon* —which still remains popular among necromancers and which has been revised innumerable times since the fourteenth century— describes a number of rituals for summoning devils. Like most works detailing the methods for conjuring demons, the *Clavicle* warns against misuse of the power of invocation. There are a number of recorded cases where suppliants, because they did not observe proper respect or precaution when invoking a devil, were brutally killed.

The *Clavicle* gives very precise details. It tells how pentacles are to be used; prescribes the ritual preparations a suppliant must observe, such as fasting and purification; advises how staffs and batons are to be made; and generally provides magicians with all that is required for the invoking of supernatural entities.

Essentially, there has never been much difference between invoking good or bad spirits. The key was in the *intention* of the suppliant. The invocation itself was a prayer and plea for aid from supernatural sources. The difficulty was always a question of definition. For example, if the magician sought alms to aid God's work among infidels, it could be reasonably expected that Christians called this good works and infidels denounced it as black magic.

Of course the invocation called upon God or Jesus, or upon Satan and perhaps some particular devil, depending upon the magician's wish and intention; but the basic supplication, like most prayers, remained fundamentally the same. The ineffable names listed in the Kabbala were used by both satanists and devouts for different ends, and presumably with different results.

Manly P. Hall, in his *Masonic, Qabbalistic and Rosicrucian Symbolial Philosophy* (1936) noted that "ceremonial magic is the ancient art of invoking and controlling spirits by scientific application of certain formulae".

It was the formulae that differed, not the prayer. Invocants seeking Satan's aid used different hierograms from those seeking God's aid. To invoke devils, for example, the symbols were always inverted. The triangle, used in divine invocations, was reversed with the peak facing downward in rites calling up devils.

Diabolic magic did not evolve rituals of its own in early times, but borrowed divine rites for the power they presumably had, and perverted them, or *inverted* them, so that the power was directed downward, never upward.

All satanic rites were left-handed, or done in a manner opposite to divine rites. The pentagram, common in all high ritual, which has historically been a five-pointed star, and which signifies the five senses of man, the five extremities of the human body, the five elements of nature, has its own special perversion to diabolists. This always differed from the divine use in one of three ways: the star was left open at one point; one point was downward, two points were upwards; or the supposedly equal points were made of different sizes.

Those who used a pentagram for divine rights called their star the Great Magical Agent. Through its power they were entitled to master all creatures its use invoked. Satanists, on the other hand, called the inverted pentagram the 'sign of the cloven hoof' or 'hoofprint of Satan'. When the star had two points up and one point down it was called the 'Goat of Mendes'. In all the perverted forms, however, a satanic pentagram allegedly granted to an invocant the same power of mastery over those whom it invoked—in this context devils—as the orthodox pentagram conferred on invocants seeking divine aid.

Many prayers of invocation appealed as directly to Satan as their opposites appealed to God; but the most common verbal invocation directed to Satan or some other particular devil, used precautionary references to some deity, even though many satanists held that devils were burned or felt pain or were forced to return immediately to Hell if the name of a Christian deity was mentioned within their hearing.

On the strength of the common invocation employing God's name being used so frequently, the following preamble is offered. For those who chose to consider themselves genuine diabolists, in common with so much in Satanism the same preamble could be used omitting the names of deities and substituting in their places the names of Satan or some particular prince or lesser devil of Hell.

> Omnipotent and Eternal God [or Satan] who hath ordained all creation to thy praise and glory and for the benefit of man, I beseech thee that thou wouldst send one of thy spirits, who shall most willingly, faithfully and readily show me those things which I shall ask, command or require of him, and truly execute my desires.

> Spirits whose assistance I desire, behold the protective aura of the very Hallowed Names of God full of power. Obey the strength of this invocation and ritual knowing I am safe in the shield of the All High. Now come out of your hidden caves and dark places, appear at my injunction prepared to serve me.

If the demon appeared the invocant then made known his desires and, perhaps, an accommodation was achieved.

The more complex invocations employed a devil's symbol as well as his name. They also employed all manner of ritualistic ingenuity such as freshly cut laurel leaves and limbs, virgin parchment, swords that had drawn human blood, inverted crosses made of cross-thorn dyed black, and red or black silk thread twisted from left to right instead of from right to left. But the basic invocation was begun as noted above, and, providing the supplicant *believed a devil would appear* and was genuinely in earnest, the assumption was that his plea would be heard in Hell and a demon would be dispatched to weigh the invocants' proposition.

In the seventeenth century a form of heresy within the Catholic Church itself—which was called Jansenism and which held that the natural human will was incapable of good—strengthened the conviction among many zealot churchmen that devils, with the secret aid of human beings, could be invoked without all the elaborate ritualism sophisticated demonologists averred was necessary; and it doubtless appeared that this was so when the vast number of ignorant, illiterate people who were served by demons became known.

On the other hand, though, arraigned witches of substance, from church prelates to knights, lords, and wealthy burghers, were not put to death until a disclosure of some kind of hair-raising black rite in which each had played a stellar role. Occasionally this same involved and secret sequence was detailed in justification for the torturing and burning of some lout or demented old woman, and, except by other ignorant and illiterate—but not stupid—peasants, it was usually believed such things had taken place even though the accused heretic neither knew the words nor could comprehend the significance, let alone read or pronounce, the lengthy invocations.

There was proof in the invocations, and the accusations against those charged with using invocations, that Satan was willing to be invoked. If additional proof had been needed—it wasn't for many centuries—sceptics had the conviction of thousands of churchmen, as well as millions of abysmally superstitious common people, not to mention great secular lords, even kings and emperors, who held an unshakable belief in Satan, the hierarchy of Hell, devils on earth among men, and the visible evil devils caused. They believed it all as convincedly as the ancient Greeks believed in that other chimera, the half-lion, half-goat called Chimaera slain by Bellerophon. It was the *belief* that fathered the fact, not the other way around.

But, diabolical invocations, being simply prayers—although beamed in the opposite direction from most prayers—never had of necessity to be any different from prayers to God; they could be ungrammatical, crude, barbarous, and even innocently obscene, as long as they were in earnest. The Church had litanies and rigid prescriptions for the faithful to follow in calling upon God, but probably more spontaneous, heartfelt and genuine prayers following nothing grander than a prayer's personal supplications, reached on high, than was the case with the other kind. The same principle obtained with respect of diabolical incantations, except that fear could induce a diabolic to be more prudent; but in both cases the paramount issue was the same: belief. Those who invoked devils and genuinely believed demons existed, were as successful as those invocants who called for angels on the strength of a similar conviction.

Satan heard invocations and responded with as much fidelity as did angels. It could even have been reasonably assumed he was *more* responsive; people had been invoking him a lot longer than they had been praying to Christianity's God.

That devils responded to invocations whether simple of elaborate was demonstrable. While churchmen, Catholic or Protestant, were very circumspect about condoning God's miracles, Satanists were the opposite. Every terrible storm or fire, all wars and plagues, were the Devil's work. In numbers, Satan worked many times over as many 'miracles' as did God. Presumably he did all this in response to invocations. Thus Satan *was* real, *would* respond, and *could* perform great feats. That churchmen made this possible by so stringently restricting God's miracles was a plain fact.

Otherwise—and this fact was largely responsible for many satanic invocations—the world for more than 1,000 years after Christ's advent, was so ordered that the only way destitute people could survive was to rob, steal, pillage, even murder, for food and for meagre safety. God's priests had denounced all these things as terrible sins. But when hungry peasants could not live unless they did them, having neither the money nor the opportunity to do otherwise, they did them. Then, guilty of terrible sins, they abandoned God from necessity and turned to Satan. As Satanists they were entitled to repeat crimes. It probably did not exorcize their inhibitions, but it kept them and their children, alive, which was important to the peasantry if it was not necessarily important to the popes or the kings.

Excluding those who invoked devils to gain additional power or wealth, the majority of invocants were concerned with vengeance, mitigation of unbearable wretchedness, all the conditions arising from penury and degradation, from suffering and affliction. It was possible, after reading even falsified confessions of condemned heretics, to understand that what had been sought, for the most part was exactly what the churches and the feudal systems had failed to supply: a living, some protection, and hope.

The Devil furnished at least the latter, and on dark nights or from an ambush beside a trail, he was liable to furnish something more tangible and therefore more gratifying—a victim to be robbed or a meal to be stolen.

Neither the Church nor respectable Christians condoned this— and while the former was quick to deny outlawry, the other, with a more direct approach, was even quicker to put transgressors to death—but if, as was often the case, a charge of Satanism could also be brought, then both Church and government collaborated in making the victim's departure a prolonged ordeal of agony.

It was common to attribute even minor mischief to Satan's influence, which implied a pact between people and devils. From this it was very easy to go one further step and impute an invocation. Hell grew in strength and influence, and its Lord increased in malevolent stature. He was available, and his legions were willing, all one had to do was offer a prayer. To distraught people one prayer must have seemed as good as another; if divine aid was withheld, perhaps diabolical assistance would not be. And to those who were not destitute but who sought greater wealth and power, things God would probably not grant, an invocation to the Devil was certainly worth the time required to offer it.

FIFTEEN

Hell in Britain

Scotland and Wales knew devils well. So did Ireland, although in earlier times Ireland held a most unique position in theological thought—but more about that later.

England—except when otherwise and transitorily influenced by such men as James I, or later by the writings of Perkins, Roberts, Cooper, Dalton *et al.*—adopted a sanguine, even a subjective, view, of Hell, Satan, the hierarchy. Most of the ideas coming over from the Continent were viewed if not with outright scepticism, then were at least considered from a standpoint that seemed to have its roots in doubt.

Laws against intercourse with devils were enacted quite early. King Ethelred in the tenth century approved a law exiling those who knew devils, as well as prostitutes. But earlier, an Archbishop of Canterbury, Theodore (668–690) legislated against Satanism in his *Liber Poenitentialis*. Punishment was usually mild, although sporadic interludes of savagery occurred, but when a Satanist *was* put to torture and death, although the punishment was indeed severe, it was actually no worse than the usual and typical punishment for any kind of criminal in those times.

It must have been frustrating for Satan to have the free run of Britain and find himself so little recognized as the cause of travail—except perhaps in Scotland where those with whom he had formed pacts were hunted down and treated with particular harshness.

For example, under English law, the rules of arraignment, the standards of evidence, and even the penalties inflicted upon Satan's human allies, followed the same course that was used against felons accused of common crimes. Satanists were seldom accorded the special treatment they got in France, Germany, or

Italy. If a Satanist, through any agency—satanic influence and assistance, or whatever—caused the death or injury of some-one, or if he was charged with having set afire a neigh-bour's rick of hay; his trial was based on what he had *done*, not on how he may have come to do it, and he was sentenced accordingly.

There were, however, some unique trials. A satanist, real or alleged, could be charged with having caused a storm, or with having caused an evil spell to injure or kill someone. Still, what the Satanist was tried for was what he had done against either another human being or his property, and the burden for the prosecutor was to prove that the accused had, in fact, actually committed a crime *against a man*. Satan or some particular demon did not directly enter into it.

It was what people *did* that got them into trouble, not what someone *thought* they might do, or thought might be behind their motivation.

For Satan, who was excluded by law, it had to be a hard blow. And if, as some authorities had claimed, Satan suffered from self-doubt, periods of dark despair, and loathing for his realm of Hell and also for himself; he must have known in addition, at least for as long as he sojourned in England, a sense of rejection and in-security.

The early English did not deny Satan or demons; they simply adopted rules that appeared to hold men responsible for what they did, the assumption seeming to be that demons, although probably quite capable of getting people into trouble, could only do so if the person permitted such a thing to happen.

Under King Athelstan (925–939) death was the penalty for murder by Satanists. It was also the penalty for any other kind of murder. England in those days—all of Britain in fact—had a fair number of people the Roman Church called pagans and heretics, believers in fen-fairies, evil boggarts and quite an assortment of good and evil spirits, and the general practice was not to observe extremes. Not long after Athelstan, the new lord of England, William the Conqueror, mitigated the death penalty to banish-ment, and still Satan was excluded; a crime was tried on its felonious merit alone.

Satanism as represented by witchcraft, continued to be rather lightly dealt with for several more centuries, although on the Continent it was vociferously and zealously denounced.

Witches and Satanists were more often ridiculed than persecuted, unless the accused happened to be a nobleman; then, because a number of uneasy kings presumed some ambitious lord might have in mind forming a league with Hell to overthrow or kill them, Satanism, necromancy, witchcraft, diabolism of any kind could be, and usually was, thought of as treason. And that kind of an accusation could be extremely painful.

Later, Queen Elizabeth, a Christian lady with a strong taint of lively superstition, considered it a treasonable act for anyone to cast her horoscope. Under Elizabeth, Satan finally achieved recognition, much later than he had managed this on the Continent. It is true that under another lively monarch, Henry VIII, a statute was enacted against Satanism; but it was repealed by Edward VI in 1547.

Elizabeth's statute of 1563 made Satan respectable in England. Thereafter trials of Satanists assumed a familiar form, beginning with the Chelmsford trials in 1566 and progressing steadily over the years. Under this statute the penalty for invoking devils was death. But, although the rules of legal evidence were occasionally waived, as in the 1582 St. Osyth trial, it remained possible for accused Satanists to win acquittal in England long after this possibility had been expressly prohibited elsewhere.

The later statute of King James I (1604) all but did away with this possibility, however. King James was—until his later years, when he performed a *volte face*—an adamant, vindictive foe of all accused Satanists. Nonetheless, even during the worst years for Satanists, which were those near the end of Elizabeth's reign, at no time were all accused diabolists put to death. In the years between 1567 and 1597, under Elizabeth, a mean average of something like 25 per cent of all accused satanists were acquitted; and if this appears a shockingly low percentage, it should be remembered that these were the decades when Satanism in England was at its most virulent, and it should also be recalled that on the Continent during those same decades not a fraction of one per cent of alleged satanists were freed.

Satanism, with a feeble toehold in England prior to Elizabeth's 1563 statute, achieved prominence afterwards; but by 1584 the debate was raging, and it would continue practically unabated for another century and a half, with Reginald Scot's derisive *Discovery Of Witchcraft* (1584) setting the course for subsequent scholars and other dissenters.

The results of outspoken scepticism, and, one may suppose, a general lack of sympathy for Catholicism, the sponsor of Continental satanism, as well as a distaste for the luridness that was supposed to accompany trials of Satanists (sex, for example, rarely got more than a discreet reference in English trials, while on the Continent it was rampant), seemed to rather well inhibit Satanism in England. But in Scotland this was not true at all.

Scottish Presbyterians were as savage and cruel as were the Germans in their persecution of Satanists. Ministers frequently conspired with secular officialdom to assure convictions, and not only did the Scots resort to torture in most cases, but they also stifled the healthy scepticism that worked so well in England to moderate this brutality.

Still, Scotland was a backwash. Its knowledge of Satanism arrived late, and although many Scots were still, by 1563, like many English, not above believing in fairies and sprites, Mary Queen of Scots made them aware of Satan's presence in that year by a statute which denounced Satanism as a crime. Subsequently these hardy, obdurate people sought out demons with a particularly—and peculiarly—Scottish zest. For example, although even in the sham trials of France and Germany confessions had to precede a sentencing to death, in Scotland a Satanist could be burned without ever confessing, if his or her reputation was thought to warrant it.

James VI of Scotland (James I of England) lent an impetus to Scottish persecution of Satanists that legitimized almost every excess that ensued. Servants were tortured in cellars and kitchens by their employers, senile and deluded people were put to death on the strength of a recommendation of a committee of eight laymen, providing at least five voted the death penalty.

In the year 1640 the General Assembly of the Kirk of Scotland laid a charge upon all churchmen to root out Satanists and see that they were properly dealt with; and the result for that year, and until about 1663, was that the worst epidemic of torturing and putting to death ensued.

A peculiarity of Scottish trials—but perhaps appropriate in that frugal locale—was that accused Satanists were required to pay the costs of their trials; and if they were menials or tenants their employer had to stand the expense.

Unlike English trials where a defence was encouraged, in Scotland, once the formal indictment (called a 'dittay') was filed, the accused could not dispute whatever it alleged. This was copied from the Continental system and ensured death, commonly by strangulation—also the Continental custom—then burning of the corpse.

When belief in Satanism waned elsewhere, the Scots still found Satan and his demons in their land. Well into the eighteenth century Satanists were in very real peril for their lives in Scotland; and although the scepticism and resistance that had prevailed elsewhere finally put a stop to Scotland's cruelty, as late of 1773 Presbyterian churchmen approved a resolution that confirmed their belief in Satanism.

Ireland was a refreshing antithesis to Scotland. In very early times, although there was a vague knowledge of Ireland, no one was quite sure of either its composition or location; it was therefore rather like fabled Atlantis, alluded to as the 'Island of Saints', and was accredited with all manner of miracles and wonders.

St. Patrick's Purgatory came in time to somewhat tarnish this idyllic notion, but for a long time the Earthly Paradise was thought to be a mystic island westerly from the known parts of Christendom: Ireland.

The Irish themselves, however, thought the Island of the Blessed lay still further westward. They had a legend of how a descendant of St. Patrick, sailing westerly to Paradise, came to a special island which thereafter went by the name of St. Brendan's Island. Some claimed the holy man had sailed *east*ward, but the general and lingering consensus said westward. It did not really matter and, even after the mystery of elusive Ireland was resolved by exploration, since it had little gold, inhospitable natives and, at least for a goodly portion of the year, an abominable climate, Ireland was allowed to return to its insignificance and its lethargy —a Christian land, but not entirely so by Catholic standards, since an occasional errant turned up favouring fairies, elves and the like.

Satan's hierarchy appeared in Ireland, but almost as an after-thought, and departed without raising much hell.

While the Continent seethed with Satanism, and even England and Scotland, in differing degrees, went about the grim business of exorcizing with Bible, rope and stake, Ireland was relatively free of the taint. In the year 1324 Bishop de Ledrede was called by the Seneschal of Kilkenny a "vile . . . interloping monk"; and eventually the Bishop himself, who tried to inaugurate an inquisition, was accused of heresy, managing to escape difficulty only by strenuous effort, but not before he had caused to be burned several alleged Satanists.

The Irish, not unmindful of Hell and its legions, were nonetheless disinclined to accredit their presence in dangerous numbers to Ireland. When churchmen would have insisted Satanists were abroad, the Irish nobles opposed them.

Aside from no more than perhaps a dozen condemnations and burnings, performed with the usual illogical hysteria, Ireland was relatively free of persecution. In the year 1447 the Irish protested to the King that not only was their land free of Satanists, but that, regardless of what was thought elsewhere, no such prevalent evil as Satanism was existent "at any time in this land".

Among those few Satanists who were put to death was one deserving attention. He was a 'blackamoor', a negro, which was in itself unique in Ireland—or England or Scotland either—in the year he was tried as a witch, 1578. Whatever the facts of his trial, he had appeared at a very poor time in a part of the world where a wicked person was known as 'black hearted', and evil actions were known as 'black deeds'. Also, quite a few contemporary pictures showed Satan as a black demon.

Of course the negro may have been a Satanist, or at least some sort of African cultist of the so-called devil-worshipping variety; but, whether any of this was true or not, it is improbable that he was a practising Christian or that he worshipped in an identical way with Ireland's Catholics or Protestants. And if he did not, of course he was a heretic, Satanist or not, and by popular opinion deserved death—and got it.

The Irish Parliament adopted Queen Elizabeth's 1563 statute (which was not repealed until 1821); but nothing very momentous came of it. The last Satanist prosecuted in Ireland went on trial in

1711, and altogether probably no more than between eight and twelve Satanists were put to death during the entire period of the Satanism-mania.

There was a good deal of dispute, and there was also some recrimination, but there was never the kind of general conviction nor the zealous resolution that obtained elsewhere. Satan was sorely disappointed in Ireland; his hierarchy, recognized only by priests, ministers, and a few laymen, was seldom invoked.

The Irish, not generally influenced by what occured on the Continent, and in former times an insular people, most certainly believed in Hell and Satan, and of course, where it was appropriate, in Purgatory; but they appeared generally doubtful of devils being abroad in any vast or serious numbers, nor did they appear from their actions to favour any extensive witch-hunt in Ireland. If there *was* a genuine Devil who meant no good, the Irish most probably visualized him in human form, as sitting upon the English throne. But basically, while it was the nature of the Scots to be fiercely uncompromising in their opposition to Satanism, and as it was equally the nature of the English to be sceptical, it was also the nature of the Irish to view without much concern, the possibility of Satan and his demons doing much harm in an area already adequately populated by waggish Little People.

The churches were strong in Ireland. Irishmen professed to be strong in their faith. But whether they were or not, there was one thing they did *not* need, and that was demons. They already had the English.

A fiend from Dürer's "Descent of Christ into Limbo"

A medieval sketch of the "Trumpeter of Evil"

Satan and Beelzebub, one of Doré's illustrations for Milton's
Paradise Lost

SIXTEEN

Hell in America

Satan arrived in North America with the first colonists, and, while he subsequently achieved some notoriety at Salem, in New York, and even farther south in Virginia and South Carolina, initially there were matters appertaining to survival that easily took precedence. This fact illustrated rather well a point it was always easy to overlook: where people were busy, Hell's hierarchy was invariably relegated to the shadows.

Subsequently, with the land under cultivation, the savages pushed out onto the distant plains, there to await the next vast westering thrust, with cities built, seaports developed, national security and personal liberty assured, it was possible for Satan to step out of his gloomy limbo.

But even then, because the actual apex of the Satanism-mania was well past in Europe, and the Age of Reason was usurping earlier churchly prerogatives, the average colonist was ready to accord Hell the variety of recognition that injured it the most: neglect based on ridicule and strong doubt.

It did not help Satan's cause, either, that the indigenous redskin population was superstition-ridden. The Europeans did not generally hold Indians in high esteem, then or later, so it was understandable that what they held in contempt among the natives, they could hardly admire in themselves. When they ridiculed the Indians' devil, who in many cases was not very different from Satan, they came away with questions concerning their own devil.

But there were among these people enough bigots—men like Increase Mather and his son Cotton—zealots, fanatics, educated psychotics, to kindle in the New World the fires that were waning in the Old World.

What occurred in America paralleled what had been happening in Europe for roughly 100 years—the diminution of the importance of Hell's hierarchy. Exorcists no longer made an issue of a demon's name, rank or status among the infernal orders. That which had been so important during the Renaissance and the Reformation had begun to fade in importance shortly prior to the close of the sixteenth century. By the seventeenth century, detailed demonology, along with much more that had once been relevant about Satanism, was well on its way into obscurity.

The Devil remained, as in earlier England, but in a collective sense: all demons were devils. They were not required to be anything further. Ultimately the individuality was all but lost—which marked a subtle, and rather imminent, departure of the entire hypothesis of Hell, and of an individual god named Satan as well.

American theologists and demonologists encountered devils whom they off-handedly called Satan. American churchmen denounced *the* Devil, but what they meant was *all* devils. When a collective definitive was required they used the names of *the* Devil; many an early-day Bible-banging, alleluia-shouting, barnstorming frontier preacher had never heard of Asiel, Asmodeus, Dagon, or any such creature as a heliophobic imp of Psellus's sixth form. They were convinced that *the* Devil existed, plagued mankind, and to him they attributed all wickedness, overworking him scandalously.

Still, the Devil's imprint in North America was neither deep nor lasting. Three dozen people were put to death as Satanists, while many more than that number were tried under a score of charges ranging from direct allegations to suspicions of diabolism. Most trials were held in the northern colonies, the English settlements, and what community fervour was worked up occurred in New England.

New York, where Dutch settlers predominated, reflected the Old World Dutch scepticism. As in Holland, New York's colonists not only refused to be caught up in the vortex—the tempest in a teapot—but they offered sanctuary to those fugitives from the sporadic New England virulence who felt impelled to flee their homes. Not always graciously, but at least without much protest.

In Virginia one Grace Sherwood was arraigned on a charge of

Satanism in the year 1706, and three years later another woman was arraigned in South Carolina, and was acquitted. Twenty-four years earlier an accused Satanist, Rebecca Fowler, was hanged in Maryland.

The southern colonies, excepting these instances and several others of even less significance, were singularly free of either alleged or confessed Satanists. But this applied only with respect of the white people. Black slaves were always suspect, and occasionally one was immolated, hanged or shot; but although these people were almost without exception heretics by almost any Christian standard, with a fair proportion probably being so-called Devil-worshippers, no one went out of his way to make an issue of this, nor to even undertake so much as a cursory investigation for the best of all reasons: slave owners had a lot of money tied up in those chattels.

An exception occurred rather late in the annals of North American Satanism, in the year 1790 at Cahokia in what became, twenty-eight years later, the State of Illinois. A slave called Moreau who stood accused of trying through witchcraft to murder his master and mistress was hanged "on a tree southeast of Cahokia".

Another slave was also executed in the same general area for alleged Satanism, according to the official journal of Colonel John Todd, Lieutenant-Commandant of the County of Illinois under Governor Patrick Henry, of the Commonwealth of Virginia, in the summer of 1799:

To Richard Winston, Esq, Sheriff in chief of the District of Kaskaskia. Negro Manuel, a slave in your custody, is condemned by the Court of Kaskaskia after having made honourable fine at the door of the church, to be chained to a post at the water side, and then to be burnt alive, and his ashes scattered, as appears to me by record. This sentence you are hereby required to put into execution, on tuesday [sic] next at one o'clock, in the morning, and this shall be your warrant.

> Given under my hand and seal at
> Kaskaskia, the 13th day of June,
> in the 3rd year of the Commonwealth
> John Todd.

It undoubtedly did not help the cause of these men that they were black, but, in fairness, neither was whiteness any warranty of leniency. The majority of Satanists put to death in America were not black. But regardless of colour, such grim punishment was usually avoided.

It was the custom among America's colonists to whip, commit to pillory, to jail, and to banish adjudged miscreants. Some alleged Satanists were treated in this fashion—which must have been humiliating to Satan, whose converts in former times had merited capital punishment amid fanfare, and this latter-day treatment was no better than a common chicken thief could expect.

Rhode Island held no trials of Satanists although there was a law on the books that would have allowed it; while Connecticut put to death, in the year 1646, a woman named Windsor, the first person hanged in North America as a Satanist. Subsequently, eight others were executed for the same reason in Connecticut. Two Swedish women were tried as Satanists in Pennsylvania—which had no statute against diabolism until 1717—in the year 1684; both were released.

Massachusetts was pre-eminent in the North American persecution of Satanists. As early as 1636 witchcraft was catalogued along with treason and murder as a capital crime. Governor Winthrop's journal noted an interesting episode in the year 1639: "The Indians near Aquiday began pawwawing in this tempest, [and] the Devil came and fetched away five of them." Evidently Hell was in need of an ethnic variation.

In 1648 one Margaret Jones was hanged at Boston as an alleged Satanist. Three years later an ill woman, Mary Parsons, accused of harrassing two other women, Rebecca and Martha Moxon, was tried and acquitted; then was remanded a second time on a charge of having murdered her own child, and sentenced to be hanged. The evidence appeared to indicate that, as in England, while Satanism might be alleged, when an accused felon was punished it was for a crime against people, not for an assumed act of heresy.

In 1655 a woman named Ann Hibbins, a widow who was noted for her temper and sharp tongue was twice tried before she was condemned and executed. At Hartford in 1662 another luckless old woman was condemned and executed. The list grew longer by the year, and drearier.

One variation occurred in Essex County in the year 1659 when an alleged Satanist, John Godfrey, of Andover, was brought to trial at Salem Courthouse, and after an initial hearing was freed on bail. Godfrey, with a boldness unheard of in Europe, inaugurated a counter-suit against his accusers charging slander, and won. From one detractor he was awarded damages in the amount of 10s. and costs (50s.). From another detractor he got 2d. and costs (29s.). This case not only proved that Satan was vulnerable, but also that barristers were not so hell-bent on getting rich in those days.

In 1673 one Eunice Cole, charged with having had sexual intercourse with Satan and found guilty, instead of being sentenced to the gibbet or the stake, was ordered to "depart from, and abide out of, this jurisdiction".

Generally, victims did not suffer unbearably. Some were sentenced to lashings and the stocks, others were acquitted or banished. In the year 1680 Elizabeth Morse, accused of diabolism, was convicted and sentenced to death. She was reprieved, not once but twice, and was released.

Even the furore aroused by Cotton Mather, America's equivalent to England's infamous Matthew Hopkins, the Witch-finder General —albeit too late, and in too poor an area for victims, to achieve Hopkins' success—was not able to re-kindle the waning popularity of Satanism although he tried hard.

Cotton's father, Increase Mather D.D., a one-time president of Harvard College—from 1685 to 1701—and a noted American churchman, was also the kind of ecclesiastic who in earlier decades in Europe would have gone to the stake as a heretic. He believed in ghosts, was able to accredit spirit voices, and had a leaning towards supernaturalism in all its forms. He was also addicted to treasonous sentiments and on a visit to England made a number of remarks that could have brought him to grief fifty years later, when sedition was unlikely to be overlooked in an American, erratic or not.

Cotton was as unique as his father, but more forceful and

vehement. He was Satan's foremost American adversary in his generation, was responsible for the infamous Salem trials, and never ceased from his denunciations even when common sense made most other anti-Satanists desist in the face of a growing and outspoken ridicule.

Cotton Mather's personal misfortunes coincided with the decline of Satanism, and he died in 1728, embittered, unregenerate, and rather generally dishonoured.

Satan may have approved of Mather's bleak ending, but if so he must also have bewailed a subsequent and somewhat simultaneous decline in his own fortunes, because no one came forward after Mather to thunder against him from pulpit and lectern.

In fact, no one after Cotton Mather ever again managed to really sound convincing about demonology in *Christian* America— not even when such things as the Ghost Dance craze of the latter-day Indians, which would have been such a welcome theme for inquisitors in earlier times, erupted near the closing years of the nineteenth century.

In *non*-Christian America, not only among the blacks who had reason, perhaps, to turn to Satan to alleviate a condition the white deities of Christianity chose to ignore, but also among the red men, in whose theologies Hell had been strong even before the first ships from Europe appeared. In fact, Indians had been burning wicked people at the stake long before this cruelty was ever witnessed in America by Europeans, although it should also be noted that this variety of treatment was never limited solely to those thought likely to be in league with devils.

Indian theology acknowledged Satan, though not by that name— and not in fact by a particular name except among particular Indians—but his demons, their influence and actions were not altogether different, nor was Satan himself so different that he was not recognized at once by the first colonists.

Durable and doughty Captain John Smith, the Lincolnshire man who was noted by historians as being the "hero of the colonization of Virginia", was quoted by Edward Arber who edited his journal in *The Works of Captain John Smith* (1884) as saying Indians worshipped the devil: "There is yet in Virginia no place discovered to be so savage in which the savages have not a religion.

Deare, and Bow and Arrowes. All things that were able to do them hurt beyond their prevention they adore with their kinde of divine worship; as the fire, water, lightning, thunder, our ordinance peeces, horses, & c. But their chiefe God they worship is the Devill. Him they call Oke and serve him more of fear than love."

Captain Smith's unfortunate use of the word *adore* is offset by the sentiment of his last sentence. The Indians feared the Devil; they did not revere him.

Even 100 years later, by the year 1707, and with reason to view askance the Trinity of Christian missionaries, the Indians were not Devil-worshippers. Another century passed and, despite some Christianising the Indians by and large, preferred their primitive pantheons—which in fact were always superior, for them, to Christianity.

The worst period for American Indians was after the advent of the second century. From 1808 until the closing years of the 1890s Indiandom suffered its most devastating reverses. Near the close of that period a Sioux said in poignant bitterness, "God has turned his back on us. He has gone to the white men and no longer cares what happens to Indians, so now we will die."

But Satan was unable to fill this void. Even though embittered stronghearts advocated Satanism from time to time, Indians were never, in general, willing to abandon their Good Spirit. Contrary to the claims of white missionaries and others, who viewed Indians as idolators, blasphemers, the worst kind of heretics, they were animists, having this in common with all primitive people. They understood the duality, but they also understood the essence of good; and if their environment and heritage made them heretics to Christians, in the contrary sense they usually viewed Christians as being much closer to being Satanists because, while Christians extolled a benign, loving God, Christian actions were very obviously dictated by the Devil.

Satan, Hell, demons and wights appeared in most American-Indian religions, as did numerous spirits whose endeavours could be both beneficial or mischievous. The legends concerning all these entities had parallels in Christianity's fables and allegories. Much that Europeans encountered among Indians was strange to them, but theologies were recognized at once—indicating, one may presume—that in spite of variants, the religion of one was similar enough to be understood by the other.

Certainly Europeans recognized Satan, his abode and his demons among America's aborigines. Europe had no monopoly, although it may have deserved one, on Hell.

SEVENTEEN

The Decline of the Hierarchy

There were a number of reasons for the decline of Hell's hierarchy, and obviously one was the great difficulty arising from the hierarchy's size. By the time Reginald Scot wrote his *Discoverie* in the late sixteenth century, it was possible to name at least sixty-seven princes and lords, the majority of whom commanded at least ten legions—most commanded between thirty and fifty legions, and a few such as Sitri, who commanded sixty legions, and Bileth, who commanded eighty-five legions, kept adding to their Orders until it was almost impossible to particularize about the hierarchy with accuracy.

Scot's figure of "14,198,580 devils", excluding the lords and princes, was derived from reliable Continental sources, but others were inclined to believe the hierarchy was much larger.

It did not have to be in order to be impressive; in those days it was numerically superior to many of the nations recognizing that Hell's hierarchy existed.

Size and complexity created a burden the secular world could have handled if there had been a valid reason, but not one the secular world had to be concerned with; that was the church's area and churchmen were perfectly willing to catalogue devils, but the flaw appeared when *only* churchmen continued to be concerned. Hell's hierarchy had become so large and unwieldy that laymen were awed by it; but, more significantly, they sought some simple accommodation, and in time that vast hierarchy churchmen had used as a tool to inspire a terrible fear, was reduced to one name: Devil. Not necessarily a particular devil—although later, as noted in North American demonology, Devil meant Satan —but *any* or *all* devils.

People were tormented, they wrote, by *a* devil. *The* Devil, meaning Satan, became representative, but in an interchangeable context; when people were required to name devils, they almost without exception referred to one devil: Satan. He became the acceptable definitive for Hell's entire hierarchy, the simplistic accommodation, and inevitably the hierarchy suffered. Churchmen had succeeded in creating such a monolithic hierarchy that they also succeeded in destroying it.

It was not a matter of people being educated beyond earlier concepts through the advent of the Age of Reason, as has been suggested. People were well along towards achieving the simplistic accommodation before that new age arrived. The hierarchy had begun to fade quite a few decades before Satanism took serious root in the New World.

The demons who had previously motivated such evils as avarice, cruelty and lust, faded almost entirely, and these vices became *principals* of evil—endemic wickedness that survived in men because men, not devils, willed it to be so.

When latter-day churchmen denounced evil they did so according to the secular acceptance of it; Satan was the tempter and the hierarchy seldom was mentioned. Satan was at work, rarely his imps. The same thing happened to Hell's hierarchy as had happened to all the old pantheons; materialism, scepticism, a passage of time in which superstition yielded to some form of philosophy of fatalism, doomed it. The metamorphosis could only be complete when metaphysics were viewed in the same context as the earlier mythologies were viewed, and this happened when science, as advocated during the Age of Reason as the real key to material salvation, managed to escape from the responsibility the early church had surrounded it with.

As for the hierarchy, which had been so painstakingly created over so many centuries, there were always enough demonologists willing to labour on its behalf to keep it alive, exactly as there always were enough superstitious people—or ignorant ones motivated by apprehension—for demonologists to influence.

The question of the nature of evil, being one of the oldest riddles known to man, in his moral, religious and philosophical speculations, always lent itself to fantasies. To people *wishing* or *believing* they might do good, only to discover after a sufficient length of time that they had in fact done evil, the plausible excuse was to blame an evil supernatural: Satan. Building on this to create an entire hierarchy of evil was not only inevitable, it was essential. In reverse, those who *knew* evil, yet still perpetrated it, as in a war to end wars, were caught between a stone and a hard place. They had to rationalize a duality, which they did, thus God and Satan became either the same or very similar. And what ensued was additional bending of the concepts of both good and evil to achieve an accommodation that was material, not abstract—and of course that was where the flaw lay for in an increasingly material existence, the choice was either abandonment of the idea of good, or an accommodation with the concept of evil. Man chose to call it duality. He could perhaps have more aptly called it hypocrisy, but in any case his hierarchy of spirits who served evil flourished, then waned when it became too cumbersome. The idea was to use the hierarchy as an *explanation* of evil, but what the church did was try to make the hierarchy the *cause* of evil. It was an example, up until the closing years of the Middle Ages, of ecclesiastics insisting that the smoke caused the fire, not the other way around.

The obvious fact, ultimately accepted by laymen, was that Hell's hierarchy, aside from being too complex for general understanding, was suspiciously like a weapon of the church, not a device sanctioned by God, and consequently the hierarchy began to lose its force and substance even among rational churchmen.

Education played a part, but only belatedly. *Rational* education was a long time arriving at the point reached by *instinctive* rationalization long before Christian schooling eased imps and devils out. Most early education was either church-sponsored or church-oriented. Subsequently, when liberal materialism worked at achieving ecclesiastical detachment, the church influence stubbornly resisted. Satan's *name* remained, even after Martin Luther's variety of Devil supposedly atrophied.

As long as the principle of evil lacked a better name, Satan's was used, and, between the adamant church view that Satan *was real* and the history of wickedness that personified him as its representative, endured, Satan could survive.

His hierarchy, however, became an anachronistic curiosity. Asmodeus, for example, along with Belial and Asiel, Saleos, Focalor, Sitri, Raum, Leraie, Gaap, and all the others, finally, after centuries of vigour, became moribund. Education, because it failed to exorcize Satan, *the* Devil, either as an entity—in parochial education—or as a principle, an abstraction in the general academic sense, did not, regardless of what educators claimed later, have much to do with mitigating, abrogating or even with castigating, *Satan.*

But education resolved the issue of the *hierarchy* by defining it as a form of medieval superstition based upon ignorant credulity—a point of view arrived at quite some time before educators accepted it by men such as Reginald Scot in 1584, Samuel de Cassini in 1505, and Andreas Alciatus in 1514.

When the hierarchy of Hell was being generally discredited by others, a number of educators were still encouraging the belief in Satan as an entity, even after Satanism as a heresy and a felony had been dropped as a crime worthy of punishment by most Christian nations. The aspects of heresy remained, but not as acts liable to secular punishment. Those thought to have sinned as latter-day Satanists were subject to church indulgences, to penances, but eventually there was no law outside the church requiring sinners to atone.

The hierarchy's demise paralleled the equally factual demise of church power. The hierarchy's demise also paralleled a far more significant demise, that of the strength of Satan's Exalted Adversary (but more of that in Chapter Eighteen). What appeared fair and just was that, while Hell lingered and Satan as the Lord of Hell continued to exist—in a weakened form, but still adequately impressive—his nether world bureaucracy did not so much fall into disgrace as fall into disuse. In a material world where less and less emphasis was placed on individual evil, and where most things from politics and religion, to commercial and industrial productivity, recognized only an equivocation of the good-bad thesis—i.e. success-failure, affluence-poverty—the change with respect to Hell and Heaven was notable for a latter-day disassociation from angelic hosts *and* devilish legions. There was God and there was Satan; good and evil. All the intermediate shades and complexities were neglected. Even if people during and after the Age of Reason, up to and including the era of the Industrial Revolution, had still believed, they would not have had either the time nor the inclination, generally speaking, to be terribly concerned.

It was not only easier to recognize a simple duality—the good and the evil—but it was also more progressive to do so, and this obtained not entirely because there grew to be more and more people—an accelerated thrust towards survival, an aggressive tendency towards equality, an enlightened urgency about industrialization—but also because, as these things became more dominant, a concept of good did not necessarily have to stand in any relationship to God, nor did evil have to be related to Satan. It was possible for the same malignancy to destroy *both* God and Satan. In fact it could be stated that if one suffered, the other one also suffered.

Commonplace materialism, the same factor that had been dethroning gods and devils since the initial fleets and caravans abetted the growth and affluence of the first great mercantile enclaves, despite churchmen or educators, despite politicians or latter-day Crusaders, freed men of their dependency on God as well as of their fear of the Devil.

Industrial 'good' became that which engendered productivity. Industrial 'evil' was that which inhibited productivity, and God had as little to do with the former as Satan had to do with the latter. Neither a host nor a hierarchy was involved, and the Church, which only lived or died, as history proved, by its toadying awareness, was perfectly willing to forget it had ever advocated the burning of hundreds of thousands of people, over anything as bizarre as a hierarchy of Hell which was presumably associated with Satanism. The day when a pope or a priest could raise a standard in God's name and recruit a host was gone long before either churchmen or educators were willing to concede this was so. Their doggedness was rooted in the isolated instances of sectarianism such as the separatist movement of America's Puritans. In these cases churchmen stubbornly clung to the promulgation of the old notions of a good God and a wicked Satan. The result was that the fundamental trinity of God, Church and Satan, suffered, and the way was opened for the enemies of all three to undertake further and fatal undermining by the best of all means —ridicule. When it was possible to make Satan appear vulnerable (and the English were particularly adept at this) he was on his way to join the hierarchy in comparative oblivion.

Science, which the Catholic Church anathematized from earliest times, eventually proved that disease was not caused by diabolical infestations, and that very efficiently did away with entire legions of devils.

Later, innovators such as Jung and Freud dealt additional, although hypothetical, death-blows to a wide assortment of devils and superstitions. "It would seem," said Freud, "as though each of us has been through a phase of individual development corresponding to that animistic stage in primitive men, that none of us has traversed it without preserving certain traces of it which can be re-activated, and that everything which now strikes us as 'uncanny' fulfills the condition of stirring those vestiges of animistic mental activity within us. . . ."

True or not, and this appears open to question, the *idea* was adequate to destroy older beliefs. Earlier, the hundreds of documented cases of diabolic possession among nuns, monks, common people and others, in which ecclesiastical exorcists struggled mightily to evict hordes of malicious demons, when subjected to rational scrutiny, turned up a wide variety of psychoses. Madness, while not always amenable to clinical explanation or treatment, was eventually acknowledged to be a form of emotional disturbance originating within people, and having no connection whatsoever with devils, although, in the frequent instances of insane ecclesiastics, the diagnosis was likely to recognize that an excessive intellectual diet of asceticism with emphasis on the struggle against devils, was certainly a cause of abnormality.

The Church fought such revolutionary ideas long after the majority of people accepted them. A general accord between religion and science was never entirely possible. Churchmen resisted the banishment of devils exactly as most of them preferred the option of a genuine diabolical entity to an abstraction called simply 'evil'.

But science, more than academe, doomed the hierarchy of Hell. Disease could in many cases be made to respond to the treatments advocated by scientists, not exorcists, and madness, which the church never managed to noticeably ameliorate with prayer, was often at least mitigated by medicine.

Even ancient and powerful Asmodeus, who throve for thousands of years because lust was not only inherent but was from time to time respectable—and pleasant—and who had never succumbed to churchmen but in fact ridiculed them to scorn, could finally be subdued by the repressions of science.

When education and religion were divorced on the grounds of incompatability, and education subsequently courted science, Hell's hierarchy was part of the settlement; the Church got it, lock, stock and barrel. Science and education, the latter coming rather late to its realizations, complemented one another, thus widening the gulf between fact and fantasy.

As far as the secular realm was concerned, the hierarchy simply could not accommodate itself. Materialism was at fault, but so was the unwieldly size and complexity of this Christian variety of animism. There was no way for a Church that almost completely lacked originality to bring its greatest creation up out of the eighteenth century into the nineteenth and twentieth centuries, with even a small degree of credibility. A few artists, and an occasional writer like Collin de Plancy, perpetuated not Satan nor his hierarchy but a myth. Their purpose, deliberate or accidental, could do no more. The eras of materialistic rationality eventually achieved an adequate impetus that had no counterpart in the ecclesiastical world—at least not in that world at the levels where policies and dictums were created—and in consequence Hell's hierarchy, because the Church stubbornly refused to abandon it while with equal stubbornness science and education refused to accredit it, found its median in the area where all fantasies and nearly all religions ultimately reside—in the often captivating, commonly improbable, between-world of mythology.

The hierarchy of Hell declined, the infallability of the Bishop of Rome declined. Satan clung stubbornly to a past greatness older than Christianity, but lost ground steadily after the advent of the free-thought epoch. Roman Catholicism in general failed to produce any defenders, biased bigots, of the stature of Thomas Aquinas after the sixteenth century, but in the lay-world men such as Newton and Immanuel Kant, among others, demonstrated where the new genius lay, and did it with such power and vigour that the best mediocrities Catholicism—and Protestantism—could bring forth could not even cast faint shadows of doubt with their rebuttals.

By the seventeenth century the destruction of deism was progressing with formidable strength. Philosophy usurped many of the prerogatives formerly held by the Church, and a few of the new breed, such as Benedict Spinoza (1632–1677) an early exponent of the fresh discipline of rationalism, called by churchmen everything from heretic to satanist, undertook to explain religion in wholly scientific terms. In the eighteenth-century Immanuel Kant (1724–1804), another of the philosophical rationalists, concluded after much study that science and religion could not be combined. Furthermore, Kant found no God in the world of physical law and no indication of immortality, so of course neither did he find a Devil there.

In Germany Kant was attacked by the Lutherans as a heretic. The Catholics were equally as vituperative in their denunciations, but Immanuel Kant was less an agnostic or atheist than was Benedict Spinoza. Kant tried to give new ideas and support to religion in the face of a growing scientific disbelief, in the only way such an accommodation could have been achieved: by bringing the stultified faith of the Middle Ages ahead into the new era, by remaking the concept of Christianity's God—the hoary, bearded, toga-clad *espiritu*—into a Universal Entity, an Almighty Intelligence.

But of Satan the philosophers as a rule had only one reference: evil. The *entity* of Satan, his invididuality, the Collin de Plancy concept, was devastated.

Of Hell's hierarchy there was scarcely a shard left. What science had not destroyed with its enlightenment, the philosophers fairly well put to death with their reason. Arthur Schopenhauer (1788–1860) held that evil arose from man's fear of death, about which he knew nothing, and as far as metaphysics was concerned, man was "satisfied with clumsy fables and insipid tales". There was no hierarchy of Hell and never had been; life was a burden and a tragedy because man was so situated and created that he could not live any other way, and it had nothing to do with devils.

A thing was not good of itself, according to Schopenhauer. It was only good because people desired it. The same with evil; if a thing was considered to be evil, then obviously it had to *be* evil. Satan had nothing to do with it, except as a definitive form.

Schopenhauer's contention that life was evil because life was strife, that it was *man's* will to survive that brought conflict, inward and outward, rather well negated the concept of Satan. All the inconvenient trivialities that beset men were entirely his own creations. He could blame whatever force, supernatural or otherwise, he chose, but the basic fact was that man, through competition and his natural needs, was entirely and exclusively the reason for whatever befell him, and the only way to blame man's evil on another form, was to believe that some variety of predetermination—a god for instance—was involved. But as long as man had an option, as long as he did not *have* to be either good or evil, that idea seemed unreasonable.

The philosophers proliferated, and they differed enormously in their hypotheses, but whatever else they accomplished, whether enlightenment or confusion; without exception, they doomed Hell's hierarchy.

K

EIGHTEEN

Decline of Hell's Adversaries

"The scriptures lay down man's moral relation in the form of history," wrote Immanuel Kant, "representing the opposite principles in man as eternal facts, as Heaven and Hell. The significance of this popular conception, dropping all mysticism, is that there is but one salvation for man, which lies in his embracing in his heart the moral maxims."

By the time Kant said this, the dissent had been growing for about half a century; and in some lands, such as England which abolished the penalties against so-called Satanists in 1682, Hell's adversaries were strong. But thirty-nine years before Immanuel Kant was born, a Dutch physician, Anton van Dale, went so far as to maintain that the evils attributed to the earlier pagans were nothing other than church fraud. Another Dutchman, Balthasar Bekker, wrote in the closing decade of the seventeenth century that a personalized, individualistic Devil was a hoax, and an unnecessary one at that. A professor at the University of Halle, a large and corpulent man named Christian Thomasius, after sitting in judgment on an accused Satanist whom he sentenced to death and who was subsequently burned, made a serious study of diabolism, came to the conclusion it was all fraud, and thereafter argued against prosecution of Satanists on the grounds that human beings could have no compact with the Devil because Satan had no bodily corporeality.

What set these adversaries of Satan apart from Kant, aside from logic, was that when they denounced Satan as an ecclesiastical hoax it was still possible to be successfully attacked by the church for doing so. In some places the Inquisition still functioned as late as the first quarter of the nineteenth century. Bekker van Dale and Thomasius spoke out much earlier.

Also, the adversaries of Hell were as divergent in their reasons as they were in their nationalities, and a large number of them were almost as illogical in denouncing Hell as their opponents were in defending, or at least in justifying, it. The trend was to dissent; even churchmen, when burning was no longer condoned, argued against a personal devil. Satan came under attack from all sides. Even a queen, Christina of Sweden, as early as 1649, issued a decree against punishing Satanists. And a Frenchman, Gabriel Naudé denounced persecution during the reign of Louis XIV; but his liberalism was denounced as heresy and the Parliament of France, convening at Rouen, refused to be influenced, and insisted that not only did Satanism exist, it deserved capital punishment. The king, however, intervened and, by royal decree of the year 1672, all Satanists to be tried were freed. (In 1683 Louis was required to reinstate capital punishment for Satanists, but limited the power of judges, so, although acceding to influence, Louis still managed to mitigate to a considerable extent the power of French inquisitors).

As Satan's adversaries grew in numbers, so did their denunciations of all things that were associated with Hell. This did not include merely the hierarchy, it also, rather prophetically, included the Church, all the Devil's advocates past and present, and finally, as rationalization spread, Hell's chief adversary, God himself. As Hell and Satan declined so did their adversaries.

The *basic* reason was materialistic scepticism, but the stated reason was opposition to a threadbare concept arising from outdated scholasticism. The Church was stagnant and had been for some time. The concept of Hell was not up-dated, and Satan as a demon-entity was still held by churchmen to be, like Martin Luther's Devil, a malicious individual. The Church was unyielding, which only added to a rather general disavowal among all people. As the strength and numbers of dissenters grew, so did the scepticism. Even a few Catholic churchmen, seeking to reach an accommodation between Rome and an increasingly hostile laity, tried to interpret papal pronouncements so that they agreed, or at least implied a degree of consent, with the widespread and growing enlightenment. But Rome denounced these men, destroyed their best efforts, and called down the wrath of God on sceptics—

who were heretics—as though nothing had superseded the twelfth- and thirteenth-century views.

As late as 1785, when things like equality, freedom, individual initiative, were being acknowledged throughout Christendom, and when men viewed Hell as well as its Lord in the light of allegory, the priest Gilbert Bauer came out with the Church view in these words:

> You know what happens when meat is salted. The salt enters all parts, every nerve and every bone, and communicates to all parts its acrid qualities; and yet the meat is not dissolved nor annihilated by the salt, but on the contrary preserved from decay. In the same way the hellish fire will enter into the innermost marrow, and be distributed throughout the entrails. It will take hold of all the arteries and nerves and make the brain boil with furious pains, without causing death or annihilation.

Another noted churchman, Dr. Justus George Schottel, said, "How much time and suffering, how much anxiety, and torture and despair, must be gone through in Hell, must be endured, borne, experienced and realized, by hundreds, by thousands, by hundreds of thousands, by millions of years in burning pitch, in flaming sulphur, in red-hot iron, in poignant blow-pipe flames, with weeping and wailing and gnashing of teeth infinite; with hunger and thirst miraculous; in stench and darkness cruelly . . . [in this] all-discomfiting, all-terrible and all cruellest infinity of hell-torture. . . ."

Hell, then, was still a place, and its Lord was still an individual demon; the Church would not relent. Only with respect to the hierarchy did the Vatican's views appear to renege, and then only by omission.

Dogmatic theologians continued to uphold a belief in a personal Devil long after doubt and ridicule in the secular world had all but destroyed him. The consequence was that the Church lost prestige, and this monolith, which had been infallible and inviolable for more than 1,000 years, suffering some earlier reverses such as the so-called 'Babylonian captivity' when the Pope held court in Avignon instead of Rome, but always able to revive and recover, finally began to lose much more than land and power and wealth—it began to lose its primacy over the minds of men. By the eighteenth century the German *Aufklarung*, the French

Encyclopaedist movement, and the English Enlightenment, had forged a very real ring of reasoned doubt around the stubborn dogmatism that was Church policy and conviction, demonstrating a very real and growing hostility throughout Europe.

The French Revolution was disastrous to Rome's hopes and plans in France. Still, the Church would not relent. As late as 1864, a papal syllabus called religious tolerance, freedom of speech, freedom of the press, liberty of conscience, secular education and separation of church and state, heresies.

If the popes had deliberately tried to alienate church followers they could not have succeeded better than they did between the years 1682 and 1864. But, as the Church suffered, and as Hell and its hierarchy faded steadily, and even Satan lost ground, so did his adversary on high. The dogmatists who could not, and who would not, recognize the need for change and progress, cast the God of Christendom in a position where He too was ridiculed. The result was sectarianism on a scale never before witnessed in Christendom. God was shaped to fit the demands and the needs of all manner of cliques. He became one thing to English Anglicans, another thing to German Lutherans, and still another thing to American Baptists, Quakers, Mennonites and Mormons.

Satan, too, suffered a divisive dismemberment. What ensued was a loss of power and prestige for both; a growth of pettiness that beggared the schism of the Reformation; a diminution of the influence of Satan's chief adversary, God. Hell's adversaries, earthly, heavenly, corporeal, angelic, real or spiritual, could not survive if Satan himself was unable to. Inevitably, to people who saw nothing to fear from Hell or the Lord of Hell, there was nothing to be feared from their opposites. The Church-sponsored crusade against evil could not avoid causing a paralleling insensitivity to its opposite. If there was neither diabolically-sponsored wickedness, nor a Devil who determined it, then there was probably no ineffable good nor a great spiritual Lord to sponsor that either, and a Church that could not come forth with an illuminating explanation was also a great failure.

The result was that, as boldness grew and the Age of Reason flourished, pragmatists like Tom Paine were able to wield greater influence on men's minds than were popes and priests, and as is usually the case, the pendulum swung too far in the other direction. Hell became less a myth than a basis for derision, Satan became a source for jokes, Heaven was termed a superstitious hallucination, the Roman Church became the enemy of all free men, the popes were incarnations of evil, and God was torn into fragments so that each group of people who still chose to accredit Him could mould Him, not into a deity but into a comforting convenience.

For example, the homespun-clad American frontiersman who left his rifle in the vestibule when he went into a church, knew that his God understood perfectly that there was no way for him to keep the Fifth Commandment. Frontiersmen killed out of hand, not solely so that they would survive but so that the things they believed in—including their church and parsons, and their God—could survive. And their God understood that this was as it had to be.

Satan's historic foes waxed and waned as did Satan. Those who had denounced him the loudest, could measure each victory by their own loss, and, ironically, exactly as ridicule injured Satan more than the rhetoric of churchmen, the same variety of dishonour and ridicule destroyed them as well. It was never enough to vanquish Hell; there had to be a relevant substitution for it. When churchmen persisted in a threadbare theology, which was not appropriate to the Age of Reason, they hurt themselves more than they hurt Hell, which was already in limbo, because they did not bring forth a substitute dogma suited to the new times.

If Satan declined, so did his foes on earth. The schismatics that came to flourish were as weak as Hell had become. Those who could no longer recall the hierarchy in detail were the same people others in the next generation could not recall either. The Campbellites came and went, the New Light Evangelicals, the Penitentes, an entire pantheon of splinter-Christians, most of whom recognized only their own God, and many of whom confused God with Santa Claus.

As for Hell, it became for these people the same tool to be used as a weapon against apostates and backsliders among their own as it had been employed in earlier times by the Bishops of Rome; it was a threat and a promise, a means for blackmailing all strayed lambs of the Lord, but only among those who could be blackmailed. All others, invariably professed Christians but in practice more like pagans or agnostics, while not easy in their minds about such a frightening concept as Hell, were also the products of eras when the latter-day sceptics had inculcated doubts the ecclesiastics had never satisfactorily refuted, so they could take refuge from Hell in all the illogic and half-truths that passed in their time for reason. But in escaping from Hell, they also managed to escape from Heaven.

Hell's adversaries could not survive their own reasons. If Hell was a place, then Heaven was also a place. But if the sceptics both within the theologies and outside of them, the advanced free-thinkers who usurped Rome's prerogatives among nations, could reason Hell out of existence, it was equally as plausible by employing the identical logic to reason Heaven out of existence. If there was no need for priests to intercede in the cause of salvation from hell's fire, why should there be a reason for priests to intercede at all; in short, what was the need for priests?

The Church's dilemma was not only acute, it was also unenviable, because, while this was the precise reason it could not and dared not relinquish its position about Hell and Satan being genuine, on the other hand, generally speaking, people no longer were able to accredit anything as perilously close to being a myth. It was a case of the trapper being caught in his own trap. There was certainly no easy answer. In fact there did not appear to be any answer at all. That was exactly where the cause of Christian theology got stalled, and there were no logicians within the theology equal to those who had augmented the fracture on the outside, or, if there were such men, the best they could have hoped to accomplish was a compromise, and no one, neither a pope nor a layman, could or would accept compromise by the eighteenth century.

The Age of Reason, reinforced by science, by education, and by those who strove to create a godless cosmogony—which was not difficult—undermined God very effectively. A reaction of outrage by itself was not enough. It never had been and it never would be. The Church's God could be challenged, could be questioned and derided, the Heavens did not fall. His word could be proved contradictory, pointlessly cruel, archaically inappropriate. Salvation in Heaven was no substitute for anguish on earth. Christ did not die to save man, he simply died; a poor fisherman, a carpenter's helper.

It did not matter to the adversaries of Hell *and* Heaven, those who usurped the role of derogators from the Church, that what had been promised by God in the Bible was man's word not *God's* word. What mattered was that 1,000, almost 2,000, years of promises were still only promises. Science did much better; it alleviated suffering and abetted enlightenment. What Lucretius had said two millennia before, about religion being the worst thing to befall mankind, seemed true.

The new-age logicians did what their devout predecessors had never done, they lumped Heaven and Hell, God and the Devil, and came out in condemnation of them all. For the first time in the entire history of man it could be forecast that entire strong nations would one day be godless, the first to destroy Hell's holy adversary since men learned to walk upright. They could destroy God with the identical logic, the same arguments, those who had worshipped the Christian God had used to destroy Hell and Satan. It was merely a question of time before it had to be done.

But the destruction of Hell's Adversary had another corollary; if nothing were substituted that could replace the *spiritual* need, the new system would also falter and fail. Science, an amalgam of that which was—earth—and that which is—man—could not achieve a similarity adequate to serve the spiritual need for very long. But that did not concern seventeenth- nor eighteenth-century man. He was intrigued by the forms and shades of freedom, physical, intellectual, and spiritual. For him the destruction of an ancient and terrifying myth was enough. If he had to sacrifice a hypothetical salvation in order to escape an equally intransigent damnation, the result was a kind of freedom on earth no previous generations had ever known, had in fact ever dared hope for. It was enough for a while and he could make such a trade with a clear conscience.

Satan could depart, Hell could dissolve, God and Heaven could go or remain according to individual conscience; what mattered was that free man was master of his universe for the first time in history. By his own effort and application he could stand or fall; the capriciousness of Devil-inspired storms and plagues could not cause terror, nor could the awesome fury of a wrathful and venge-

ful God. Hell's adversaries, through their own professed association—their enmity notwithstanding—could not survive that which
they had struggled so long to overcome.

Those who did not rest until they could vanquish a world were
also the victims, and if there was no way for them to come out of
a confining medieval intellectualism, then very possibly that was
where they should have remained, frozen in a frame of time that
belonged to them exclusively—they, and their Devil and his Hell,
their God and His Heaven.

NINETEEN

Ridicule

About the year 1855 in Lancashire, England, when a number of card-players continued their game through Saturday night and into Sunday morning, a stranger who joined the game had an extraordinary run of luck. When the stranger casually crossed his legs the other players noticed that he possessed a cloven hoof. They fled in all directions.

In Germany quite a bit earlier Satan accosted a farmer demanding half of each crop the farmer planted for three years. The terrified farmer asked which half Satan desired. After deliberating Satan said he would take the upper half. That year the farmer planted potatoes. The next season Satan said he would take the lower half and that year the farmer planted wheat. When the third season arrived Satan demanded half of whatever grew, and the farmer let his fields lie fallow and only weeds grew.

It was a very long time before people dared ridicule Satan, but a few brave souls took chances in the sixteenth century, although as a rule when they used a demon as the butt of their derision he was usually not *the* Devil, but *a* devil.

Only when the common dissent encouraged people to general and outspoken ridicule did *the* Lord of evil, Satan, finally fall so low that even countrymen ridiculed him. But obviously, ridiculing Satan could lead to derision of other supernatural entities, but that was a different matter, worthy perhaps of additional discussion elsewhere.

By the latter years of the seventeenth century several books by dissenters achieved popularity, and the common trend, when the real danger passed, was to relate instances of Satan being outwitted.

In England, for example—where it was alleged that 'raising the devil' could be accomplished quite satisfactorily by simply reciting the Lord's prayer backwards—near the village of Blackburn a pair of farmers at the chore of flailing grain decided to break the monotony by trying an invocation. They recited the prayer backwards, and at once a fissure appeared in the barn's earthen floor and Satan pushed his head up, then his arms, but as he prepared to climb completely out, the astonished countrymen overcame their shock, and beat the Devil over the head with great vigour, using their flails, until he departed amid much howling. It was, actually, a lot of unnecessary exercise. The English believed that to dismiss devils all one had to do was make the sign of the cross and speak aloud the name of Jesus Christ.

The Devil, for some obscure reason, took up residence in the English village of Cockerham, so the legend went, and harassed the people to such a degree of exasperation that at a public meeting, called to discuss means for ridding themselves of Satan, it was decided that the schoolmaster, a learned man, should undertake an exorcism.

Having, at some trouble and after several days of diligent application, discovered how to raise Satan in order to banish him, the schoolmaster, properly at midnight, went through a diabolic ritual. Satan suddenly appeared, but the schoolmaster, "when he saw his large horns and tail, saucer eyes and long claws . . . became . . . speechless".

But even in a situation as portentous as this one undeniably was, no schoolmaster was ever speechless for long; and when Satan demanded to know why he had been summoned, the schoolmaster told him it was the wish of the good folk of Cockerham that he depart and never return. Satan agreed to depart providing the schoolmaster could set him three tasks which Satan would not perform; but if he succeeded in accomplishing these tasks, not only need he not leave Cockerham, but also, the schoolmaster's soul should be his.

Upon ratification of this proposal by the schoolmaster, the Devil was given his first task: he was to specify the exact, correct number of dewdrops upon a nearby hedge. Satan had no difficulty at all, and accomplished this within moments.

He was then assigned his second task, which was to count the number of stalks within a certain field of grain. As before, Satan accomplished this within moments.

The third task was put in the form of doggerel: "Now make me, dear sir, a rope of yon sand, which will bear washing in Cocker, and not lose a strand."

Swiftly Satan went to work twisting up a rope of fine sand. He gave it to the schoolmaster, who went at once to wash it in the river, but it could not stand the washing, so "the devil was foiled, and at one stride he stepped over the bridge over Broadfleet, at Pilling Moss" and disappeared, never to appear at Cockerham again.

Tailors, it would appear, gave Satan a particular amount of trouble. At Chatburn, in Lancashire, when the Devil cajoled a tailor into a trade similar to the one he offered the Cockerham schoolmaster, the tailor's last wish was that Satan should ride . . . "back to his quarters on a dun horse, never to plague him more", and the Devil, perceiving that he had been outwitted, "gave a yell which was heard to Colne," as he was carried away to Hell astride a dun horse.

What, one was entitled to wonder, had become of the omnipotent and omniscient Devil of earlier times?

Another tailor, this one in Germany, caused such turmoil in Hell it was commemorated in a poem:

> A tailor went to wander,
> On Monday, in the morn,
> And there he met the Devil,
> His clothes and shoes all torn.
>
> Hey, tailor, follow me!
> In hell the boys need thee;
> For thou must clothe the devils
> Whatever the cost may be.

The tailor obligingly went to Hell, but in the fitting of his new clients he caused such anguish with his scissors and needles, his ill-fitting garments, his punches and pinches, that the devils voted never to accept another tailor in Hell.

A blacksmith was also proscribed, according to Grimms' tales. Christ granted this particular smith a wish, and the smith asked only that he might have Satan, lord of the devils, helpless upon his anvil. It was done, and Satan was so badly frightened at the prospect of being pulverized that when he escaped and returned to Hell, he posted an order that when the blacksmith died he was not under any circumstances to be admitted to Hell.

Dunstan, an abbot of Glastonbury who later became Archbishop of Canterbury, was at work at a forge creating a Eucharist chalice when Satan appeared to harass him. The abbot seized his tongs from the fire and grabbed Satan by the nose with them.

His audacity was also commemorated in verse:

> St. Dunstan, as the story goes,
> Once pulled the devil by the nose
> With red-hot tongs, which made him roar
> That he was heard three miles or more.

Most of the tales relating how people bested Satan evolved from rustic humour. Also, as the pastime of ridicule grew, quite obviously the fearful and exalted Devil of former times—who was a personage of awesome power, a genuine deity—had to be reduced in size, in genius, and in power, until he was as poor a creature as those who ridiculed him. From the bully he had to become the bullied. The impressive *Satanas* of early times who challenged God himself in Heaven and was so well exemplified by Doré, as a huge dark, muscular and malevolent image, so frightful even in art people cringed, had to become no larger than a man, sly but gullible, petulant enough to howl his exasperation when outwitted, and in general a contemptible dimwit who only *thought* he was clever.

He could no longer use magic to injure people, nor to successfully further his schemes. He only retaliated with a howl, as when St. Dunstan pinched his nose, and reacted with petulance when the schoolmaster at Cockerham got the better of him with the rope of sand.

Playwrites, authors such as Goethe, Baudelaire, Gautier, Stevenson, Mary Shelley, Stoker, Pushkin, Poe, Hawthorne, Washington Irving, *ad infinitum*, used him, or a variation of him, as their synthesized concept of evil in near-human, or outright human, form; but in every case he shrank, lost most of his evil genius, and became at his best susceptible to a stake through the heart, and at his worst, vulnerable to the bucolic cleverness of louts.

In Germany, at Kleinbautzen, a miller tied him to a water-wheel and nearly drowned him. In Egypt, where Satan had been gathering up infidels and others and putting them into a sack which he carried slung over his shoulder, a holy man, St. Medard, encountered him on the shore of the Red Sea, and, pitying the motley accumulation in Satan's sack, slit it and freed the prisoners. Their escape was described in the *Ingoldsby Legends:*

> Away went the nice little Cardinel's Niece,
> And the pretty Grisettes, and the Dons from Spain,
> And the Corsair's crew, and the coin-clipping Jew,
> And they scamper'd like lamplighters over the plain!

Many years ago in Switzerland, near St. Gotthard, a shepherd enticed Satan to build a stone bridge over the Reuss chasm. Always available for an enterprise that would allow him to acquire a soul, Satan agreed upon the condition that he would be allowed to possess the first user of his bridge. The shepherd agreed, Satan built the bridge, and the shepherd drove a chamois over the bridge. In his rage Satan seized the little animal and tore it to pieces.

This was another of the Grimms' tales, and it very competently implied how low Satan had fallen; for although his magic and skill were adequate to complete a difficult engineering feat, the building of a stone bridge above a river, spanning a gorge of pure rock, neither his magic nor his intelligence were equal to the task of outwitting a shepherd, or exacting vengeance for being duped.

There were also many cases of Satan being bested through divine intercession, but in later times at any rate, shepherds and tailors and schoolmasters preferred to outwit Old Nick without that kind of assistance—the reason being that the same doubt and ridicule they had evolved for one deity, was also applicable to the other deity. Not, perhaps, in the same degree, not even as outspokenly nor as popularly, but with an equal, if more circumspect, validity.

The advent of enlightenment was based upon, and in fact insisted upon, man being the master of his fate as well as his world. God was as unwelcome as was the Devil. But, even though science, education, increasing freedom, affluence—general materialism—pushed God to the background; since people still knew nothing of the afterlife and feared death as they always had, and it was generally thought God had something to do with eternity and salvation, He would not be as completely derided as was Satan. At least not until another few centuries had passed after the Grimms' era.

He *was* ridiculed though, and the most prevalent—and enduring—form of derision was blasphemy. Although it was said that those who took the Lord's name in vain would suffer terribly, blasphemy became and remained the most common variety of profanity; obviously people no longer took God's threats any more seriously than they took Satan's malevolence.

As time passed God, although commonly invoked, particularly by churchmen, was not as a rule disdained by people who challenged Satan; but when the mortal triumph was achieved little if any of the glory went to God. Legends arose in which men actually succoured God and angels. A number of fables told of God and man, as equals and conspirators, devising stratagems for humbling Satan, so it began to appear that God was also being pulled down to human size and frailty, in accordance with the concept that what happened to Satan also happened to his adversary.

Men not only derided their ancient deities, they scolded them. Also, they tolerated them, but with man, not the supernaturals, as master. They ridiculed and bullied them, and sometimes they even chastised them as though they were naughty children.

St. Cuthbert, the patron of Hexham and Newcastle, who died on 20th March 687 and who was born about 635, the one-time Bishop of Lindsfarne and patron of Durham, and whose earthly travels after his death were more extensive than during his life, had a habit of returning among men for centuries after he died, righting wrongs, offering theological instruction and harassing demons.

During England's feudal period a knight, Sir Guy Le Scoope, invited a large number of people to a banquet, but because the messenger who was to convey Sir Guy's invitations failed in his duty, no guests arrived, although the great banquet hall was made ready. Sir Guy's exasperation was so acute that he called upon Satan and his hellish host to come, eat, and to carry away what food they did not consume.

No one believed any such event would occur, evidently, because when Satan, or a facsimile, at the head of a vast assortment of imps, wights, and nasty-looking little elementals abruptly arrived, Sir Guy, his retainers and most of his family sprang up and fled, leaving behind Sir Guy's infant son and heir. A demon at once seized the child. Other devils ate ravenously, ran round the room howling, leaping, destroying things, and creating a general pandemonium. Sir Guy, in great anguish over the fate of his child, cried out to St. Cuthbert, who had at the time been in his grave more than half a millennium, but who, nonetheless, suddenly materialized, and in righteous anger cowed the devils, forced them to release the child, then gave the ma good scolding, sternly admonishing them as though they were capricious children:

"... be moderate, pray—and remember thus much,
Since you're treated as Gentlemen, shew yourselves such,
And don't make it late. But mind and go straight
Home to bed when you're finished—and don't steal the plate,
Nor wrench off the knocker—or bell the gate. . . .

The demons, "fell tooth and claw on the victuals. . . . All scrambling and scuffling for what was before them, no care for precedence or common decorum," while St. Cuthbert "Took up little Le Scoope and walk'd coolly away".

From dimwit, the Devil had descended another rung to become a boisterous, obstreperous and obnoxious fool, an entity with no more prestige than a common imp. He could be given a figurative shaking by the grizzled shade of an ancient monk. And, although it perhaps escaped theologists at that time—as it escaped others, scholars as well as ecclesiastics, much later—what had happened to Hell, its hierarchy, and the lord of both, was that they had become hardly different at all in the eyes of Christians, from the oldtime Greek gods, who were also thought of in terms of human likenesses and who were denounced, berated, scolded and ridiculed for their vices, weaknesses, and demonstrable intellectual adolescence.

By the early nineteenth century Satan's prestige and magic were gone—which was no great loss. What happened in the *Ingoldsby Legends* at the manor of Sir Guy Le Scoope, epitomizing Satan's descent, though, had its implied corollary: a sceptic might wonder how long it would be, before a similar episode would evolve during which God and angels were scolded or admonished by human beings; they were equally as vulnerable as were devils. Ridicule, when it was turned upon any theology, good, bad, pagan, or non-pagan, was a powerful weapon, one against which no religion ever managed to devise an adequate shield.

Ridicule arose from scorn as well as doubt. By the time men could jostle Satan with impunity, they were able to scorn God as well. Sufficient time had passed, and no hellfire had erupted, volcano-like, to consume to ash all who scorned the Devil, and no blinding bolt of divine lightning had struck to death those who doubted or ridiculed God.

The jokes at God's expense became common. They did not proliferate as did the jokes at Satan's expense, but by the nineteenth century most people had heard them; and while some of these jokes attributed a kind of rough and humorous wisdom to God, others were, like the jokes about Satan, forms of ridicule based upon a familiarity undreamed of during medieval times.

God and Satan, who had been able to awe men for thousands of years, shrank, paled, retreated, and yielded much under the increasing scepticism of the new ages, but they, at least, were already half myth from the beginning, and therefore could quietly and conveniently withdraw to await the next epoch. But the Church was earthly substance and it could be completely devastated and destroyed by ridicule, with far less chance of ever reviving.

L

TWENTY

Fate of the Imps

The subtleties of theology and the refinements of metaphysics, which were both creative and destructive, both good and bad, were the dominant forces on earth among men for thousands of years before any science worth the name appeared; and even after, theologists could, and did, form religions suitable to specific times, particular people, even local ecologies, without consulting or considering science.

Religion was not responsible to science, nor could science prove that it should be. When science was applied to the fields of faith it faltered as it did in no other application. The early scientists, who were essentially thinkers, metaphysicians, including Kant, could seek definitions of a divinity commensurate with the capacity for comprehension in specific ages, and as long as nothing more intangible than other human beings supported, or derogated, their hypotheses, the arguments never ended. Science could neither prove, nor disprove God.

Science, theology, metaphysics, any of them, any combination of them, or all of them in consort, could at their very best theorize a god or a devil. The latter two, theology and metaphysics, had been doing that for more millennia than anyone could recall. They had been borrowing from one another, synthesizing, moulding, shaping, and sustaining, until a variety of passably interchangeable devils and demons had come into existence; and if a man defined Satan and only other men disputed the definition, his definition stood an excellent chance of achieving some degree of acceptance, large or small, over the centuries.

But if Satan *appeared* to correct the definition, tangibly and visibly, then, obviously, Satan could not only be correctly defined, but he existed. The same with God. Philosophers could speculate without end—in fact the entire substance of philosophy was an open-ended discussion—and if no deity appeared to substantiate or alter common concepts, all the metaphysicians—Kant, Schopenhauer, *et al*—could propound to their hearts' content and the nearest anyone could come in refutation would be to offer a fresh theory.

So it was when the pantheon, or hierarchy, of Hell was denounced. Everyone, churchmen, leaders, lords, and laymen, scorned imps. Neither Satan nor any of his lords, not a single fiend of substance, came forward, not so much to defend Hell or its bureaucracy but to correct the spreading conviction that there was no such place and no such hierarchy.

Learned men began rather early in the Western world to question the validity of Hell; but not until it became unlikely that dissenters would be punished did Western man really scoff and by then he had his best arguments organized. Hell and the Devil had to be pure myth, said the logic of an enlightened age, for although both were being continually maligned, not a single imp came forth to challenge or to correct the new conceptions.

There was no retaliation; the skies did not turn black and spew forked lightning, dire malignancies did not strike down sceptics, ravishing pestilences did not come to blight the world.

People, human beings, had never accepted for very long anything they could not see or touch, hear or smell, and when the churches decided to allow Satan and Hell to rest in limbo, as long as there was no one to rescue them, no prelate to thunder against them or point out visible evidence of their wickedness, it was fairly easy for common people to very nearly forget them. A reasonable result was for rational man to accept an increasingly prevalent notion that there was no such thing as Hell, and that being so, since Hell was the hierarchy's home, then neither was there any such thing as a devil, a wight, a demon, or an imp, whatever earlier generations had preferred to call them.

Obviously, early historic personages—whether theologians or metaphysicians, philosophers or other precursors of scientists such as learned alchemists—had been incorrect.

In order for anyone to refute the deep and spreading doubts, proof was needed. Not the word of the church, nor even the biblical quotes of God. As in the case of the Devil, if no one came forth to offer visible, tangible proof that the demons existed, then rational man was unwilling to believe they existed. This applied to devils *and* gods. It was substantially the basic conviction of the rationalist era; if a thing could not be seen, heard, felt, it did not exist. Anything that was not explicable in orthodox materialistic terminology, did not exist; and if doubt were based, as it always was, upon the silence that followed scepticism, and no one broke that silence, then doubt could very easily become conviction.

In this way Satan waned and God faded, but the imps proved they were still around. Two notable faiths—Catholicism, and the latter-day theology whose members referred to themselves as Seventh Day Adventists—acknowledged the presence of devils. To the people of these religions spiritualists were victims of devils. When entities manifested in visible form, or spoke audibly while invisible—commonly in seances but just as likely during the research of various reputable psychical research institutions— those devouts did not scorn the evidence as most rationalists did, they acknowledged the spirit voices and forms; but they saw these 'ghosts' not as the spirits of the dear departed but as devils seeking through diabolism to convince researchers that they were dead friends or loved ones. All this was in order to gain followers for spiritualism among the living, in a manner of recruitment for Satan only a little different in practice and no different at all in intent, from the evil diabolism of medieval times.

In one respect these Catholics and Adventists were more rational than the majority of other 'rationalists'. They sifted the evidence and found that conscious fraud was responsible for only a small percentage of the spiritualist phenomena. By whatever definition— spirits, demons, astrals, ghosts, imps—these entities did exist. That they could single out a living individual, recall some very private episode from the life of that person with absolute fidelity, was proof to these people that the hierarchy had *not* been vanquished, but that it had moved into a new era, a fresh phase, and that its power was as great as it ever was.

The premise was reasonable. Even science had proved that astral entities did exist; but science was far more cautious than was theology. Science could not satisfactorily explain poltergeists; but, through rigid—and sceptical—observation, scientists had proved that poltergeists were not myths. Psychic phenomenon, although perverse enough not to be dependable, had been demonstrated to exist innumerable times under laboratory conditions.

The general disfavour that had attached itself to spiritualism encouraged strong doubt concerning its validity, but the proofs, if not the explanations, were adequate to suggest that in fact there was *some* kind of communication possible between human beings and those whatever-they-weres.

The doubters—that is, those who did not deny the existence of phenomena—used the identical arguments to prove that they were demons that less positive researchers use to prove that there was, in fact, *some* kind of evidential spirit—commonly, the phenomena communicated with human beings. This fact had been demonstrated without any possibility of fraud too many times under the most rigidly controlled conditions to allow for honest doubt. Where the demon-theorists departed from the scientific position was in their contention that since these discarnates were capable of wickedness, as in the case of destructive poltergeists, they obviously were not angels, and therefore they had to be demons. Also, and in support of the negative view, it was suggested that since earliest times man's knowledge of ghosts had left him fearful, not entirely because of contact with the unknown but because of the traditional evil acts of these entities. Historically, ghosts had not been of benefit to people. Not all had been harmful but enough have been, to inspire a healthy dread and aversion.

Those who conscientiously could do so denied that there were such things as discarnates for as long as it was possible to cling to such convictions. When it was verified by scientists—and an impressive array of quite prominent ones over the years—that there *were* these entities, and that they were often unpleasant, or at least disconcerting, it began to appear that those earlier authorities who had taken credit for the destruction of Hell's hierarchy had done so a bit prematurely.

It appeared that the hierarchy was not vanquished after all, that what the authorities who had contended otherwise had actually accomplished was an adjustment, an accommodation; and, if one cared to do the research to prove it, an excellent case could be made for the demons, because throughout all history Hell's viability, the capability of devils to adjust, had been their strongest and most demonstrable virtue. If the most compatible way for imps to contact and influence twentieth-century human beings was through spiritualism, it could hardly be expected that they would not avail themselves of the opportunity. Nor would such an adjustment offer obstacles; imps appeared as animals, humans, and shades, thousands of years before the sophisticated religions evolved. Ghosts as wicked devils were common even in biblical times, and earlier.

Also, the world of spiritualism was obviously as well-populated as Hell had been. Almost anyone desirous of doing so could contact a compatible spirit. Because of this proliferation, and its numerical similarity to Hell's hierarchy, those who chose to believe discarnates were in fact evil imps, could point to this additional similarity as as additional proof of evil duplicity.

Also, because the validity of spiritualism depended upon belief, and the best spiritualists were emphatic in contending that unless a person was sympathetic there could be no contact, it was easy for those who considered spirits to be imps, to use the same argument; the great churchmen of earlier times were equally as emphatic in claiming that only faith enabled people to know gods—or devils.

There were a number of documents attesting to Satan's failure to pervert people who did not believe in him. With little effort these were resurrected as further proof that diabolism was endemic in spiritualism, i.e. if a person did not credit devils they would not appear to him. It was the same thing spiritualists claimed— thus the spirits conjured by latter-day spiritualists, were demons.

Science was unable to prove that spirits were good or evil, it could only verify that such things *did exist*. Theology, not restrained by the laws that restricted science, could employ all the logic of biased ecclesiastical philosophy to prove that spirits were imps of Hell in a fresh form.

For spiritualists and scientists the means for refutation did not exist. Any frightening apparition, whether it actually accomplished evil or not, usually terrified its beholders. They were willing to believe the worst because of their dread. Spiritualists and scientists, even had they the statistics to prove spirits were in the great majority of cases harmless, were nevertheless unable to explain anything else about them. All that was known of a certainty was that they *could* appear, visually or audibly. How or why this was done, no one could explain. It was impossible, therefore, to refute the allegation that spirits were actually devils seeking to retain, and to extend, their influence—as they had done hundreds of thousands of years earlier, but in a compatible, modern way.

Those who opposed this view of modern spiritualism being reincarnated Hell, had weak arguments, but this was primarily because they had so little knowledge of their subject; and just enough mischief ensued from spiritual contacts to make even the best of the weak arguments vulnerable.

Not everyone adopted this view of spiritualism being an updated form of Hades. Even some churchmen, the most notable one in America being the Reverend Arthur Ford, were convinced that spiritualism was a means for bridging the abyss between this life and the next one, and saw in it very little that had any corollary to the common concept of *either* Hell or Heaven.

Still others, who acknowledged the reality of spiritualism, saw in it nothing more than a fascinating—and at times frightening—novelty. These were commonly the same people who scoffed at the idea of Hell and imps.

What prevented Catholics and Adventists from carrying their condemnation to the extremes earlier zealots had enjoyed—burning people who spoke with spirits—was that very few people outside those two faiths were sufficiently interested to care whether a spirit who appeared at a seance was an imp or was dear departed Uncle Ned. Most people were not convinced spiritualism was not all hoax, and those with open minds did not particularly care whether it was a hoax or not. They treated it with the same neglect that had been so fatal to Satan and the earlier hierarchy, with the difference that this time the hierarchy, if that was indeed what it was, did not pass into oblivion.

The fate of the demons, then, at least in the view of several millions of contemporary human beings, has not been as unfortunate and calamitous as it would seem. They may not have succumbed to an age of reason, an epoch of enlightenment, a period of inspired rationality; they may, in fact, have not had to be resurrected at all because they may never have perished.

If this is so, then the best logic of the sixteenth-, seventeenth-, eighteenth- and nineteenth-century sceptics, while it abetted human emancipation in so many admirable ways, only succeeded in encouraging scepticism and cynicism towards Hell's hierarchy, without actually injuring the imps at all—beyond requiring that they adapt to the new eras, which they may have done in such a way that anyone seriously wishing to contact devils in this twentieth century could conceivably do so without having to cast any traditional spell at all, but by simply attending a spiritualists' conclave.

At least this hypothesis is currently supported by many ecclesiastics. They forbid the faithful to have anything to do with spiritualism; and their admonitions are like an echo from the Middle Ages. They see Satan at work, not *again*, but *still*. If it comes as a surprise to most dwellers in the twentieth century to learn that what has generally been thought of as an unattractive fragment of Western history—the medieval era of Satanism and witch-burning—survives into their own time, they might be able to rationalize that although *material* progress has been consistently miraculous, *spiritual* progress has been stagnant as a direct result of this same materialism.

But whether the discarnates of spiritualism are imps or not— and until a time when enough is known to categorize the varieties of these entities—there remains the question of their *purpose*. If they *are* imps, then of course they in all probability will work as tirelessly as demons have always laboured to dupe mortals, by whatever means are required, i.e. pretending to be departed friends or relations, saints, leaders, influential philosophers, which is the contention of some churchmen. But if they actually *are*, as that oldtime psychic sophisticate St. Paul implied when he noted that physical bodies were "raised [to become] spiritual" bodies, then the dead departed—mischievous or not, occasionally obnoxious, troublesome, or benevolent and helpful—would seem to bear out the spiritualist's claim that life and death are separated by a very minor, almost a casual, difference. And that viewpoint can hardly find much favour with churchmen either.

In the interim—which is the current time—before factual revelation, scientific or otherwise, proves that spirits are one thing or another, the imps are evidently safe.

TWENTY-ONE

Hell in the Twentieth Century

The imaginative interpretation of a phenomenon may be wrong, but the reality is there. In other words, spiritualism's phantasms may not be imps or even departed mortals, but science—leaving theology out of it—can prove that they are there.

Medieval Satanists believed in their Lord of Evil. Christians believed in a Devil that walked abroad. And both imagined or visualized him as fearsome, horned, scaly, taloned, or in the guise of an ordinary man, while in fact he need not have been any of these things, although *evil existed*.

The temptations of a St. Anthony could have been the result of obsessions of the flesh, hallucinations, bad dreams; but the *physical anguish* was real. The legends of Satan siring himself into the genealogy of noble families did not have to be anything but legend, as with the Angevins, but there definitely were great lords motivated by nothing more exalted than unmitigated evil.

In former times people accredited Satan with attributes that very few modern men believe he possessed; but he obviously *did* possess powers of a material kind, and he certainly had emissaries roaming the world. Undoubtedly many people signed pacts with him, and there have always been people willing to serve Satan and to profess themselves as either inhabitants, or associate members, of Hell. The question was: where did fact end and fantasy begin?

The issue in the twentieth century is the same as it was in the sixteenth century: is Satan an individual or is he a name used in a collective sense to symbolize or represent all evil?

Obviously, many people still consider him an individual. In the year 1926 the priest of Bombon, France, near Melun, the Abbé

Desnoyers, was flogged by local citizens because he had allegedly undertaken, as Satan's advocate, to work evil upon a Madame Mesmin of Bordeaux. The Abbé Desnoyers accomplished his long-range *maleficia* by sending demons disguised as birds, over the Mesmin residence. They carried the spawn of a disease which afflicted Madame Mesmin. It was an acknowledged fact—in 1926—that when a priest sold himself to Satan he became much more powerful than an ordinary Satanist.

In 1968, at San Francisco, California, sceptical but sincere invocants conjured up a genuine devil by very painstakingly casting an ancient spell for that purpose. They spent many days preparing for this event, and one entire sleepless night in performing the ritual. When the devil appeared, seven people saw him and attested to the appearance of astonishment he evinced; but before he could be approached he arced like an electrical crossed-circuit and disappeared.

The floggers of Abbé Desnoyers and the experimenters in San Francisco were positive in their convictions. The Devil existed, not as an allegory but as an individual.

In the twentieth century a resurgence of Satanism, arising in part from a dissatisfaction with orthodox Christianity, has strong parallels with old time paganism, when the unabashed and healthy delights in the pleasures of the flesh and the natural beauty of this world, stood opposed to the asceticism of Christianity, which advocated the mortification of the body to save the soul.

Two thousand years of gloomy damnation in this world, and a corresponding exaltation of the value of some future paradise, appear to have just about run their course. Modern hedonists have chosen to reject the unfairness of Original Sin, substituting in its place the permissive society and Hell has as little to do with it as has Heaven.

Those who choose to flog priests or to evoke devils are perfectly free to do either, but the majority of people in the twentieth century neither fear nor adore a good or bad divinity.

In the twentieth century Hell appears acceptable only as an abstraction, as the fleshless skeleton of an historic hallucination. It serves as the source for fictional entertainment, only rarely earning genuine ridicule, probably because the majority of people cannot be that serious about it. In the contemporary context there is less disenchantment than there is weariness with the entire subject of Hell.

In 1970 a Calfornia newspaper noted that the cult of Satanism had increased spectacularly from a negligible 1,000 to 2,000 diabolists in the previous decade, to an "alarming" 20,000 Satanists by the year 1970.

Twenty thousand Satanists, or even 100,000, out of a total state-wide population of over 20 million Californians seems hardly to qualify as an 'alarming' percentage. Assuming that the number of Satanists will multiply in California, as in Wales or Eire or Normandy, the percentage of diabolists in relation to almost any total population will not be 'alarming' in the twentieth century for the reason that Hell as a focus of interest, general, casual, or academic, cannot compete successfully with the fresher and more exciting scientific accomplishments such as walking on the moon, and other even more spectacular material achievements certain to come within the next thirty years, or by the end of the present century.

The argument about Hell's validity, like most discussions that touch upon philosophical topics, not only fails to appeal to pragmatists in the twentieth century, over whose heads is poised the distinct possibility of a very real cobalt cataclysm, it even seems adolescent in comparison to the adult horror that has a more real and imminent hold on the mind—and the imagination—of mankind.

A drum-thumping poltergeist or a shadowy materialization of some notable discarnate like the Dark Lady of Bognor, retains an equal interest in the twentieth century as in former times, but with the difference that in former times, in a less hectic and hurried —or worried—world, people's interests were less likely to be diverted by scare-headlines in the morning paper. Whether a ghost appeared or did not appear, and whether a spirit was an imp or some form of thought-projection, whether the hoary legend of Hell as a phenomenon was perhaps wrong in one sense and right in another sense, was of more interest in the nineteenth century than it could be in the twentieth century.

As religion has suffered throughout history at the hands of materialism, so does Hell presently suffer, with the distinction that because the twentieth century is a materialistic apex, Hell has deteriorated to a degree never before met with in history; from a vast kingdom of darkness second in size and importance only to Heaven itself, Hell has become, in the closing decades of the twentieth century, little more in the minds of men than an expletive denoting disgust or annoyance.

The historic conceptions not only could not have retained relevance, they could hardly even have maintained plausibility.

The idea of Hell being beneath the earth, or located on a mystic island west of Ireland, or even in the sun, fell before the impersonal calculations of exploration and science. But the most sanguine result of this revelation was that when the old legends were destroyed, at least part of the *fact* of Hell was also destroyed for progressive and sceptical mankind; i.e. if Hell was not where it had been thought to be, then quite probably there was no such place as Hell. Everything has to be *somewhere*. If it is not, then obviously it is nothing. It does not exist, or at least this was the rationalist dogma capable of arising from Hell's diminution at the hands of the doubters.

There was recourse to argument, naturally, Mystics of ancient times with the leisure for such intellectual callisthenics as cosmological philosophy, could—and did—spend entire lifetimes seeking answers to interesting abstractions, but in the twentieth century there are few groves and vineyards for sandalled mendicants to wander in eating fruit and expounding lofty thoughts.

Modern man cannot afford the time, nor does he appear to especially care that Hell may exist, or that the discarnates of spiritualism are demons who may actually live in a real Hell. Nor does he seem too concerned that if this is so, then Hell was never in any of the places history assigned it, but was possibly a separate and distinct dimension, a different sphere, another plane, another place.

The spirits *are real*. All doubt and ridicule can accomplish, now that science has proved that spirits exist, is to appear fallaciously and unrealistically stubborn in the face of known fact.

Since the spirits are real, then reasonably, where they reside, the environment they inhabit, is also real. If they *are* imps, then their habitation is Hell. Not the Hell of medieval times, but more nearly the Hell of myth, which was a separate world, a different dimension, an often vague, unrecognizable, even an unrealistic, place.

The feasibility that 2,000 years of Christianity could be half right, and the much older pagan theologies could also be half right, aside from perhaps settling an old question, would point to an uncomfortable fact: after all the persecutions, murders, inquisitions, theological perversions since Christ's advent, the Western world knows no more about Hell in the twentieth century than it knew in the first, and during that lengthy interregnum the best minds of Christianity were incapable of resolving what was a primary and vital concern of Christian theology.

If Hell is in fact another place, then the opening sentence of this chapter is valid: the imaginative interpretation of a phenomenon may be wrong, but the reality is there. All that mankind has thought of Hell may not be correct, or at least may not be totally correct, but Hell as a place, is there. Yet in the twentieth century this issue does not require a revelation. Mankind has progressed from fear and belief to wonder and doubt, to scepticism and ridicule, and finally, to general indifference and apathy. If Hell is 'out there' the fatalism that comes from indifference is able to reject or to accept it, without being very greatly concerned either way.

In a world whose problems are vast and nihilistic in nature and where the great majority of people know little beyond suffering and deprivation, a concept of Hell, of any unpleasant place, is less likely to be a source of dread than a source of irony.

Even a fresh version of any traditional Hell that has been updated to suit a sophisticated era, because of its abstract nature, would have difficulty competing with the factual misery of the corporeal world, and the old theological ploy of blackmailing backsliders with a fear of Hell could not succeed with hungry or desperate people in the twentieth century any better than it succeeded in the sixteenth century.

Hell could actually exist somewhere, and a traditionally materialistic Western world that has been becoming increasingly apathetic towards abstractions for more than half a century—since 1917, the year of the Bolshevik Revolution, the culmination of an era of general theological rejection—could hardly care less.

If this attitude causes despair among soul-saving zealots and traditionalists, it can be justified on the grounds that the Hell of history is an incongruous place, that even churchmen have been unable to identify it with modern man's knowledge and beliefs, and the brilliant artistry of Gustav Doré has reduced it to the level of science-fiction.

When accommodating theologians seek to adopt Hell to the twentieth century by interpreting the hair-raising oldtime legends as metaphorical symbolism, they rob Hell of its intrinsic terror; they dilute the purpose of Hell, which has historically been to appear so frightening that it inspired—at least theoretically—a genuine and lasting goodness in men.

The moment a priest or parson offers an apologia he destroys the image. An appeal for goodness for its own sake was never a rousing success, and a weakening of the retributive concept detracts from the fear of retribution.

The matter of traditional Hell being re-moulded to fit the twentieth century is a hopeless undertaking. Nevertheless, this is the course orthodox churchmen follow. It has been adequate up until the nearly-godless twentieth century because there were never before entire godless nations, but now there are.

Not only godless nations, but whole areas of the world, Christian and non-Christian, whose inhabitants cannot identify with traditional faiths, because, in part, it has not been possible for more than a generation to define evil. What was once an elemental fact of life—that neighbouring states were usually enemies—has, for instance, evolved into an essential interdependance, and that is only one of the changes endemic in the twentieth century.

The church's concept of Hell is basically the same as it has always been, but neither conditions nor men are the same. What is visible and audible, what constitutes the present, is so different from the past, even the relatively recent past, that no institution from those times can make the transition unchanged. Even updating a hypothesis could only succeed providing its original thesis was demonstrably and factually based; otherwise a fresh and, most importantly, a relevant idea has to be posited. Not a patchwork Hell with its historic and archaic barbarities and absurdities, but a concept acceptable to an increasingly militant and dissatisfied world whose population has become preponderantly young.

The latter part of the twentieth century has seen the inauguration of such radical change in the hearts and minds of men that it ranks historically with any era in history that has engendered change. Hell, if it exists as a place and not as an allegory, requires a re-definition. The historic adaptability of demons, even though it has been successful for centuries, faces its greatest crisis, now, because the element that made both demons and their adaptability possible in the past—superstition—has suffered drastically at the hands of psychiatry, psychology, and science. The same obtains with the theory of Hell; it will survive providing the historic continuum as scrapped and a fresh relevance can be proved—which will not be easy in an era when no one, priests, politicians or scientists, seems to know what the needs are for the times, nor what is the destiny of man, in the closing decades of the twentieth century.

A common concept of Hell, having to do with an individual's capacity for creating his own on earth—an idea as old as fatalism itself—has gained adherence in the twentieth century exactly as it did during feudal times when people of wealth, power, substance, derived comfort from the idea that wretches caused their own wretchedness, which is a placating thought, when otherwise the deprivation of less fortunate people is a constant rebuke.

But fatalism, like agnosticism, is not an answer; it is an attitude, a variety of negativism that declines, for whatever reason—indifference, inability, incoherence—to contribute towards any understanding. Fatalists view misery on earth as inevitable. They could be correct but the simple acceptance of a fact in no way explains the purpose of the fact. Whether man creates his own Hell, or whether Hell for an individual is a matter of conjunctivity is as open to discourse as is any other aspect of Hell—or Heaven—god, devil, or man. For those to whom the ancient ideas are unacceptable, perhaps some personalized form of Hell-on-earth is satisfactory. Perhaps in an age when it is almost impossible for most people to revere a god or to fear a devil; an age when the continuing stress has been upon man as arbiter of his own destiny, Hell-on-earth may achieve some prominence, but obviously, whatever theorem finds favour, has within itself that old duality—the aspect that is acceptable, and the aspect that is contradictory.

It has been suggested that what may prevail is some kind of total rejection arising from material facts that seem both immutable and terminal. It cannot escape the starving person that his genuine anguish is not of his own doing, therefore it must be the doing of his god. If the world will not feed its inhabitants, those who go hungry cannot be expected to see themselves at fault. God or Devil, Heaven or Hell, must be relegated a continually less important position, and may very probably earn an eventual total rejection. Not that this is any kind of an answer, but if man is to be his own source, his own inspiration, his own arbiter, he undoubtedly can accomplish that which is to be done far better by rejecting that which is superstitiously crippling, than by trying to live with archaisms that so far have not helped him achieve very many of his real, and requisite, goals.

Particularly is this true if the world population can double within thirty years, or by the end of the twentieth century.

If it appears an incongruity to lump over-population with an idea like Hell, which is older than any current civilization or nation, it might be noted that nothing which is considered crucial to the biped species can be viewed in a modern context unless it is done so against this very real, very imminent, very human dilemma. The best of all arguments favouring Hell-on-earth may be no more distant than the year A.D. 2000.

TWENTY-TWO

A Modern Hierarchy

For as long as primitive man feared other carnivores he evolved and perfected rituals to protect himself from them. He also created spells whose purpose was to be destructive towards them —destructive towards *all* his enemies.

When his weapons improved to the point where he could kill his enemies with minimal personal peril, he no longer needed the protective rituals and spells. He could abandon them, and he did abandon them.

When his survival depended upon crops, he devised a system of obeisance to spirits of the sunshine, the rainfall, late frost, a bountiful earth, even to a harvest moon. When technology usurped the position of much of the oldtime guesswork, man abandoned his bucolic gods as well.

When the first animal could be effectively controlled, the need for a hunter to spend dawn and sunrise atop a hill purging himself in order to entice God's favour when he went forth, waned, and when this mastery changed the outlook of man so that he became separate and distinct among the animals, became *the master of animals*, instead of as before, just another animal, his religion's attitude towards animals subtly changed. From an importuning hunter who as often as not prayed to animal gods, man became a warrior-hunter whose paintings and carvings showed that the animal, no longer revered, had become his means for transportation or like the trained dog, an extension of his hunting, his coursing skill, but in any case, was no longer propitiated, unless in a preservative rather than destructive context.

With the cultivation of grain man coerced nature in a manner similar to the way he had mastered animals: he used his knowledge of the behaviour of each, to achieve a material benefit. With

M

nature, man learned the seasons; when to plant and when to harvest, when to expect an end to frost and a beginning of the rains. Nature, though, gave man his greatest travail—primarily because she was not only capricious, never totally predictable, but because she was very complex. Man yielded up his nature-gods only very slowly and reluctantly. They were, in fact, the last earthly gods he abandoned.

But he did abandon them; he abandoned all the natural gods. Rain, sunshine, good soil, high germination, low yield, good or bad crops, and weather, became, after something like 5,000 or 6,000 years of recorded history, segments of, not necessarily a predictable panorama, but at least of an environment that was amenable to control. What was needed was more study, less superstition, more pragmatism, less faith, more man, less god.

Within a degree of tolerance it was always possible to predict the outcome of situations and conditions, providing one employed the specifics that had been proved reliable through experience. For example, the victor in an equal, armed contest, fought upon a plain or steppe, was the host with the best cavalry; or a bountiful grain crop was assured providing it was planted ahead of the warm rains, in loamy, rich earth; or, with no understanding of the cause or purpose of a raging, communicable pestilence, it was possible to escape, to survive, by flight culminating in seclusion and isolation (obviously, a bad thing was abroad; experience showed that those who hid, survived).

What all mankind's slow progress tended to prove was that, although there was much good, at least much survival, in the world, the most notable events were the disasters. Rome was thousands of years abuilding, but Venice, which was older, could sink beneath the sea in less than a century. Good was there, but evil was just as likely to prevail, and if one had the time, without much doubt one could also witness the end of Rome. In other words, providing one used the specifics that had been proved reliable through experience, one could, within a degree of tolerance, predict things with a fair level of accuracy—and, without much exception, most predictions, accurate and inaccurate, would be bad, and they would have nothing to do with a god.

At least they would have nothing to do with *good* gods, which is the only kind of god Christianity favoured, although not everyone agreed concerning what was good; but that, in the twentieth century, was one of those pointless hypotheses, and twentieth-century man was as little likely to be trapped by open-ended philosophical discussions as he was unsusceptible to entrapment on the existence of God. But there was an undeniable fact: evil existed. Even those to whom a sanguinary sophistication was all-important, could not ridicule evil out of existence. At one time, in the thirties it could have been done, perhaps; in that decade evil coincided with bad economics. No one thought there was anything worse than a financial stricture, not in the thirties, and by the sixties and seventies when people knew better, knew that a world-wide economic depression, could be *good* not *bad*, if that was the worst condition people could invoke, it was too late to invoke a depression, or to change the definition from bad to good.

The issue was even more basic; it had to do with the abandonment of gods. For thousands of years man conjured them by the score and the legion. In shorter epochs he began divesting himself of them, but, having had hundreds of gods, meaning hundreds of reasons for believing in gods, and because abandonment had to evolve from change. And change for mankind was slow, the actual abandonment was an almost painfully tardy process, and when it culminated, finally, in a spreading kind of mindless atheism, what remained after the gods were gone, was evil.

The Devil *was there*. Not in a resurrected form, most certainly not in an original form, not even necessarily in either a modern or traditional form, hypothetical, rhetorical, or symbolical, but evil was discernible. After God was put aside Satan in one form or another remained. Five thousand years of creating cosmogonies followed by 1,000 years of theological turmoil in which genuine doubt existed and grew, which culminated in something like one century of scepticism when the habit of shedding gods continued, all this fairly well divested Western man of his traditional deities. They were no longer needed; like a dim-age spearman who killed his first sabre-toothed tiger at 30 yards with an arrow loosed from a fresh innovation called a 'bow', the need for old prayers vanished with the discovery that technology—the proper name for those specifics that made prognostication possible—was an excellent replacement for the God no one was so sure even existed.

The abandonment of old gods neither faltered nor ceased, and

Christianity, which slew the old pagan gods so zealously, also established the rules by which all gods could be destroyed. One failing of monotheism was that with only one supreme God, it was vulnerable. Unlike the Norse god, Balder, killed by a dart made of mistletoe, who was replaced in the pantheon; Christ had no understudy, and Christianity, with one Supreme God, was liable to the very rules it had established. It suffered, and it still suffers.

There is more to the fact of evil than its existence. If God is abandoned, is said to have 'died', and entire generations have matured in the twentieth century ridiculing even a theory of divinity, it simply proves gullability, something that has never required proving, while at the same time a combination of this same gullability and an acceptance of religious disbelief prove that stupidity can triumph any time and any place people by the millions breed up the numbers alone and not the quality of their species, otherwise intelligence would have rationalized long ago, that if God is dead and evil predominates, then whatever co-exists with evil, and which succours and salvages even when evil is at its most vigorous, cannot be bad, must be beneficial, good, and therefore, since good, or survival, cannot derive from bad, evil, and nihilism, obviously there is both a God, and a principle known as good.

If modern man cannot rationalize adequately to understand that sophisticated evil is nothing less than the identical, age-old *maleficia* of Hell, then neither can he understand that because evil has endless variety, there is still at work a hierarchy of Hell.

Bibliography

Bibliography

Eliza M. Butler, *Ritual Magic*, Cambridge University Press, 1949.

Montague Summers, *Witchcraft and Black Magic*, London, 1945.

R. Burton, *The Anatomy of Melancholy*, Everyman's Library, New York.

G. deGrillot, *Witchcraft, Magic and Alchemy*, Courtney-Lock London, 1931.

Satan, A Portrait, London, 1946.

John Milton, *Paradise Lost*.

E. A. Wallis Budge (Ed.), *The Book of the Dead*, University Books, New York, 1968.

Sir James Frazer, *The Golden Bough*, MacMillan Co., New York, 1951.

R. Lowe Thompson, *The History of the Devil*, Kegan Paul, London, 1929.

P. F. Waterman, *The Story of Superstition*, Grosset & Dunlap, New York, 1929.

Holy Bible, Old and New Testament, plus various addenda.

John Lord, 7 Volumes, *Beacon Lights of History*, W. H. Wise Co., New York, 1921.

C. F. Keary, *Outlines of Primitive Belief*, Scribners', New York, 1882.

James H. Breasted, *Ancient Times A History of the Early World*, Ginn & Co., New York, 1935.

John Harland and T. T. Wilkinson (Ed.), *Lancashire Folklore*, Frederick Warne & Co., London, 1867.

Philip Myers, *General History*, Ginn & Co., New York, 1906.

Russell Hope Robbins, *The Encyclopedia of Witchcraft and Demonology*, Crown Publishers, New York, 1970.

Hill and Williams, *The Supernatural*, Hawthorn Books, New York, 1965.

R. F. Davidson, *Philosophies Men Live by*, Henry & Holt & Co., New York, 1958.

G. Rawlinson, *Religions of the Ancient World*, Scribners', New York, 1883.

Manly P. Hall, *Masonic, Hermetic, Quabbalistic, & Rosicrucian Symbolical Philosophy*, Philosophical Research Society Press, Los Angeles, 1936.

Additional references pertaining to particular subjects were consulted, and in fact over the months involved in researching this book the number of sources grew and grew until a complete record would be tediously—and pointlessly—out of proportion. For those wishing to go further, any comprehensive city library should be adequate, although it proved easier in my experience to research almost any specific topic dealing with Hell, than Hell itself. Of Satan there are a number of excellent biographies, of various demons there are vignettes, but of Hell specifically, excluding mythology, there is not a whole lot.

For the Catholic view on most issues covered herein, the *Catholic Encyclopedia* is excellent. It is verbose, biased, rather antique in thought and theme, but well worth reading.

Index

Index